Historical Perspective
and International Relations

Historical Perspective and International Relations

A Collection of Articles

Yoav J. Tenembaum

Matador
Unit E2 Airfield Business Park,
Harrison Road, Market Harborough,
Leicestershire. LE16 7UL
Tel: 0116 2792299
Email: books@troubador.co.uk
Web: www.troubador.co.uk/matador
Twitter: @matadorbooks

ISBN 978 1805140 917

British Library Cataloguing in Publication Data.
A catalogue record for this book is available from the British Library.

Printed and bound in Great Britain by 4edge Limited
Typeset in 11pt Minion Pro by Troubador Publishing Ltd, Leicester, UK

Matador is an imprint of Troubador Publishing Ltd

To Mabel for her love and wisdom

Contents

Chapter 2
The Role of History in Shaping Foreign Policy

Chapter 3
Theory and International Relations/Diplomacy

Chapter 4
International Law and Diplomacy

Chapter 5
Theory and History

Preface

The collection of articles in this book, which were originally published in various newspapers, magazines and journals between 2009 and 2022, cover a wide-range of topics relating to the study of history and international relations. Short in length, the articles are aimed at a wide readership, interested in history and international relations.

Divided in five separate sections, the book highlights some of the most momentous events in modern and contemporary history having an ongoing effect in the way international relations have evolved. Cardinal events in the history of international relations are assessed with historical perspective.

The book also dwells on the role of history in the shaping of foreign policy. Some articles are devoted to international relations and diplomacy in their more theoretical aspects. A section is dedicated to international law and diplomacy, presenting articles on some of the events in diplomatic history that have wielded an influence on the development of international law, as well as advancing a personal credo on the role of international law. The book ends with articles on imagination and the study of history, on the use of counterfactual history as an additional tool to comprehend better not only what might have happened but actually what did happen, and on historical truth and historical narrative.

These articles afford an analysis of events and personalities from the perspective of a student of history and international relations. As a lecturer in international relations, who combines in his lectures the historical and the theoretical dimensions, I have tried to present in this book a similar combination of history and theory. The overview of history and international relations at the general and conceptual levels is matched by the assessment of episodes and individuals at the particular and chronological levels.

Thus, for instance, the reader will find articles ranging from the historical turning point in Russia's post-Cold War foreign policy to the role of the diplomat in the modern era; from Britain's appeasement policy towards Nazi Germany in 1938 to the role of history in the shaping of foreign policy; from Israel's bombing of Iraq's nuclear reactor in 1981 to the conceptual framework to analyze a United Nations Security Council resolution; from Winston Churchill to the use of imagination in the study of history; and from Richard Nixon to the difference between risk and uncertainty in international conflicts.

The book, through its articles, attempts to combine the rigor of academic thought with the style of analytic journalism. The book, in a sense, is an intellectual hors d'oeuvre, a brief journey into the realm of history and international relations.

Chapter 1

History in Perspective

How the 2008 Russo-Georgian War Forever Changed Russia

Putin's Russia has striven for security, influence, and stature. In trying to achieve those objectives, Russia has been ready to display ruthlessness and ignore niceties.

Yoav J. Tenembaum

The recent developments between Russia and Ukraine are only a reminder that Russia's foreign policy in the post-Cold War era could be divided roughly into two periods: from the end of the Cold War to the outbreak of the Russia-Georgia War in August 2008, and from then onwards.

The war between Russia and Georgia in August 2008 was a turning point as it projected a new assertive Russian policy beyond its borders. Two further military interventions followed, each one in a different geopolitical context and under different circumstances: the 2014 incorporation of Crimea and involvement in the revolt by Russian inhabitants in Eastern Ukraine and the direct military intervention in the Syrian Civil War from September 2015.

To be sure, August 2008 may be seen as a turning point in Russian action, though, conceptually, the roots of this new assertive policy could be gauged before. Russia had already made clear, prior to its military intervention against Georgia, that it was dissatisfied with the prevailing international order. Thus, for instance, in a speech he delivered at the Munich Conference on Security Policy in February 2007, Vladimir Putin, Russia's president, came out clearly and unequivocally against the prevailing international order, criticizing, among other things, the United States for its excessive use of force and its tendency for domination.

Certainly, from a Russian perspective, Russia's policy could be seen as reactive. The United States and its European allies had pledged at the end of the Cold War that the North Atlantic Treaty Organization (NATO) would not expand eastwards beyond Germany. The Soviet Union and Russia subsequently had consented to the unification of Germany, to the process leading to parliamentary democratic systems in formerly Communist countries, and to the consequent disappearance of the Warsaw Pact, among other reasons, on the reassurance that NATO would not extend its membership to East European countries.

That pledge was broken. So much so, that countries bordering on Russia like Poland, Ukraine, and even Georgia were offered to be members of NATO. Even membership of the European Union was regarded by Russia as potentially menacing, entailing, beyond the political and economic agendas, also a security dimension.

Such a process was perceived by Russia as dangerous. Not only was a major pledge broken, but

Russia was treated as a second-rate power, whose position could be blatantly ignored. To be sure, this was not merely a matter of status and honor. Although the Cold War was over, and thus Russia supposedly should not have worried that an eastward expansion of NATO might pose a danger to its national security, the Russian leadership still perceived that as a threat. Why?

History might give us an answer. After all, Russia had been invaded from the West by several enemies, including Napoleon's France at the beginning of the nineteenth century and Germany in World War I and in World War II. Russia had always felt vulnerable. Defensible borders for Russia had always meant a secure geopolitical sphere of influence. That could emerge either in the form of direct control, as it happened during the lifetime of the Soviet Union, or indirect influence, as it was expected would happen in the post-Cold War period. The latter, the Russian leadership would argue, did not occur due to broken promises and a lack of sensitivity to Russia's national security interest. To contend that Russia's neighbors do not harbor ill intentions towards it may be important, but ignores Russia's subjective perception, shaped by a painful history of threats and invasions from the West.

On the other hand, Russia's neighbors, used to intimidation and subjugation by Russia for centuries, perceived Russia's actions from 2008 onwards as menacing and destabilizing. Rather than wanting to be reassured about its security, Russia has pursued a policy of expansion, wishing to thwart any political move that is inimical to its worldview. Russia is afraid of its neighbors establishing a stable, thriving parliamentary democracy, and joining other fellow democratic countries in various international organizations, not because it feels threatened, but on account of its paranoid attitude and authoritarian worldview. Russia's leader, Vladimir Putin, is a modern version of Russia's Tsar, according to this assessment.

Did the war against Georgia in 2008, and the ensuing policy pursued by Russia in the international arena, signal the beginning of a Tsar-like or perhaps even of a Soviet-like foreign policy?

The war against Georgia in 2008 was a watershed in Russia's foreign policy as it translated into action a conceptual worldview that had gradually emerged a few years before. In Georgia, Russia was confronting not only a focused challenge to its friends and allies in South Ossetia and Abkhazia, but also more widely what it perceived as a threat to its international status and national security interests by an ever-expanding NATO and, to a lesser extent, the European Union.

For the first time since the end of the Cold War, Russia projected its power directly and forcefully beyond its borders (if one does not include its military incursions into Chechnya, which anyhow Russia regarded as an integral part of Russia). In responding to the Georgian military operation in

South Ossetia, Russian troops counter-attacked not only in South Ossetia but went on further to conduct military operations in Georgia itself.

Russia's victory in the war afforded its political leadership confidence and a sense of purpose.

Vladimir Putin, who thought that the collapse of the Soviet Union had been a tragedy, wanted Russia to become a superpower bereft though of the ideological drive that characterized the Soviet Union. Thus, Russia had no intention to be a revolutionary power in the guise of the Soviet Union, Nazi Germany, or Napoleonic France. Certainly, it lacks the ideological vision of a revolutionary power. Few if any are examples of revolutionary actors bereft of a strong ideology shaping their actions. Putin's Russia has striven for security, influence, and stature. In trying to achieve those objectives, Russia has been ready to display ruthlessness and ignore niceties.

Originally published in The National Interest, April 23, 2021.

How Napoleon's Legacy Explains the Middle East's Conflicts

Two hundred years ago Napoleon Bonaparte died, leaving an enduring legacy in international relations: The revolutionary power bent on altering considerably or destroying the prevailing international order.

Yoav J. Tenembaum

The latest violent conflict between the Hamas and Palestinian Islamic Jihad and Israel has highlighted the importance of understanding the conflicts in the Middle East from a status quo vs revolutionary actor perspective.

Two hundred years ago this year Napoleon Bonaparte died, leaving an enduring legacy in international relations: The revolutionary power bent on altering considerably or destroying the prevailing international order.

There are two kinds of actors in the international system: Status Quo and Revolutionary. The former accepts, more or less, the existing international system as it is, while the latter rejects the prevailing legitimacy of the international system and seeks to alter it considerably or to overthrow it entirely.

The French Revolution and Napoleon Bonaparte are the first manifestation of a revolutionary actor in modern history. The revolutionaries behind the French Revolution of 1789 tried to export its ideas to other parts of Europe, both through the pen and the gun. Napoleon's France expanded much further, destroying the classical balance of power that had existed for most of the eighteenth century.

The Soviet Union was a revolutionary power from its very inception, calling for a change in the prevailing international order. Its leaders truly believed that, following the Bolshevik Revolution in Russia, which brought the Communists to power, many other countries in Europe would follow suit.

Nazi Germany was a revolutionary power, seeking to destroy the prevailing international order.

The difference, in this regard, between the Soviet Union and Nazi Germany was that the first was not suicidal whereas the latter was; Nazi Germany took its ideology to its most apocalyptic extremes, the Soviet Union had a sense of limits.

The contrast between a status quo and revolutionary actor applies as well to sub-systems of the international system.

Thus, in a sub-system like the Middle East, the current Iranian regime can be said to have revolutionary foreign policy goals, leading it to seek major changes in the region, including the destruction of Israel as a sovereign state. The Islamic Republic of Iran is a revolutionary actor as it has striven since 1979 to alter considerably the prevailing order in the Middle East, leading former foes in the region to establish tacit or open alliances in order to thwart the intentions of the Iranian regime.

Fidel Castro's Cuba was likewise a revolutionary actor, hoping to advance the cause of marxism in its diverse radical forms both in Central and South America and beyond, as in Angola and Mozambique. His efforts to intervene in Angola and Mozambique in the 1970s to help Marxist guerrillas, in addition to similar efforts undertaken throughout Latin America, make Castro's Cuba a revolutionary actor in the international system.

Sovereign states are not the only revolutionary actors. Organizations such as Al Qaeda and the Islamic State are revolutionary in nature because they seek to overthrow the existing international system and its underlying norms. In the context of sub-systems, organizations such as Hezbollah, Hamas, and Palestinian Islamic Jihad in the Middle East can also be described as revolutionary.

What matters in this regard is not necessarily the ability of these states or organizations to implement all their objectives, but rather their intention and willingness to do so.

Thus, neither Hezbollah nor Hamas may be able to realize their respective dreams, but their aim remains the same: to overthrow the prevailing order in the Middle East – the first by facilitating a Shia-dominated structure led by Iran and the latter a Sunni-dominated Islamic sub-system in the spirit of the Muslim Brotherhood. Both entail the disappearance of Israel as a sovereign state and the transformation of the existing Arab regimes.

Israel and most Arab countries are, on the whole, status quo actors. They face these revolutionary actors the way previous status quo actors did in the past, either by attempting to accommodate them or by challenging their expansionist objectives.

To be sure, this pragmatic posture is not devoid of ideology. The fear of an Iranian Shia-dominated Middle East is regarded by the Sunni Arab world also as an ideological menace. The disdain among many Arab leaders for Hamas, an organization related to the Muslim Brotherhood and strongly supported by Turkey, has to do with its ideological tenets, which are regarded as a threat to regional stability.

The fear of revolutionary actors, founded upon pragmatic and ideological premises, has led to the forging of a tacit alliance between Israel and many Arab countries against the Iranian regime and its regional allies. It has also led to a common front against Hamas.

In this context, rhetoric has to be taken with caution. Arab leaders, including those of the Fatah-led Palestinian Authority in the West Bank, may voice their support for the Palestinian Arabs under Hamas rule in Gaza during a violent confrontation with Israel. However, the Hamas, as well as the Islamic Jihad, are perceived by them as dangerous organizations that ought to be weakened, if not altogether destroyed.

Indeed, the Hamas-Israel conflict should be understood also in the context of the bitter rivalry between Hamas and the Fatah-led Palestinian Authority.

To be sure, none of those status quo actors in the Middle East has become Zionist. They simply see Israel as a militarily strong, economically vibrant, technologically advanced, and diplomatic influential status quo actor, sharing the same view of Iran and its allies, as well as of Hamas and Turkey.

The blurring of distinctions in this context can be unhelpful in trying to devise a coherent policy. Revolutionary actors cannot be placated, only deterred. Status quo actors are prone on occasion to see revolutionary actors as rebellious status quo actors, seeking to redress a wrong done to them by unconventional means.

Certainly, neither revolutionary nor status quo actors are monolithic. Some of the first may be more revolutionary in intention than others and some of the latter may be more satisfied with the existing international system or sub-system than others. A dose of nuance is called for.

Two hundred years after the death of Napoleon, his legacy, in various forms, remains very much alive in the international arena – especially in the Middle East.

Originally published in The National Interest, May 24, 2021

Does the Congress of Vienna Deserve to Be Remembered as a Refuge of Reactionaries?

Yoav J. Tenembaum

Two hundred years ago the Congress of Vienna was held. It opened in September 1814 and closed in June 1815. It was the biggest diplomatic gathering ever held until then. Its objective was to shape a new international order following the French Revolutionary and Napoleonic Wars that had beset Europe for the previous twenty-two years.

The image of the Congress of Vienna had been tarnished by many historians who had seen it as a reactionary diplomatic exercise aimed at restoring the *status quo ante* that had prevailed prior to the French Revolution in 1789. Further, the "Dancing Congress," as it had been referred to, was, according to contemporary critics and future historians, nothing but a grand, vacuous, social gathering that failed to address the evolving challenges of nationalism and liberalism.

This view of the Congress of Vienna and the post-Napoleonic settlement was challenged by historians and political scientists such as Edward vose Gulick and Henry Kissinger, among others, who claimed that a balance of power system and a stable order emerged in its wake producing an unprecedented period of relative peace in Europe.

To be sure, the post-Napoleonic settlement was not aimed at restoring the *status quo ante*. It certainly did not produce a geographical and political map which was identical to that existing prior to the French Revolution. In this context, one should distinguish between setting an objective to go back to the *sense of stability* that preceded the Revolutionary and Napoleonic Wars and wishing to restore the *precise conditions* that prevailed then.

Suffice it to look at a map (both geographic and political) of Europe of 1789 and to compare it to a map of 1815 to realize that the latter is quite different from the former. Further, even in France, where the Bourbons were restored to power, a written constitution was introduced limiting somewhat the power of the King and securing political and civic rights unknown before the French Revolution.

To take an analogy from the game of chess, the architects of the post-Napoleonic settlement were intent on playing chess, following pre-determined rules of the game, but they did not revert back to the chess game they were playing when the French Revolution erupted.

Thus, they wanted to restore the *diplomatic modus operandi* and the *underlying political assumptions* of the pre-revolutionary era. However, they did not attempt to re-build edifices that could not be restored.

True, territories were exchanged without much regard for the national or ethnic backgrounds of their inhabitants. However objectionable this may seem to us, in the 21st century, it was certainly less so in the early 19th century. The notion of balance of power, which was embraced by the principal statesmen at the Congress of Vienna, entailed the exchange of territories and populations as a compensating factor. The belief was that a satisfied country would be less inclined to question the validity of the settlement thus reached, enhancing the prospect of stability in the international system.

Anachronism is an obstacle that one must overcome in assessing historical events. Whatever their failings, the architects of the post-Napoleonic settlement were intent on securing peace and stability following many years of wars and upheaval, which they all identified with the French Revolution and Napoleon Bonaparte. Thus, to expect them to have embraced the ideas espoused by their enemies, as they saw it, would have been absurd.

To be sure, the Allies were not a monolithic force, espousing the same beliefs. The British, an island with a parliamentary tradition and a constitutional history, were averse to seeing in every revolution the enactment of the French Revolution, as the Continental powers were. The British were certainly less inclined than their Continental allies to consent to armed intervention in order to put down any such revolution. Whereas Austria, Prussia and Russia perceived any revolution occurring anywhere in Europe as a menace to international stability, Britain considered only an attempt at exporting the revolution *beyond the borders* of the country in which such a revolution took place as a threat warranting intervention.

However imperfect the Vienna settlement may have been, the fact remains that it reflected the basic assumptions of a generation of statesmen and diplomats whose main objective was the creation of a stable international order. Certainly, they were not particularly optimistic about the prospect of peace. The Congress of Vienna Secretary, Friedrich von Gentz, for example, thought that peace was secured for around five years. Viscount Castlereagh, Britain's Foreign Secretary, hoped that peace might last ten years.

There was not to be a major European War for almost a hundred years.

Originally published in History News Network, December 7, 2014

Germany's Declaration of War on America Changed World War II – And World History

Nazi Germany had no sense of limits. That led it to invade the Soviet Union and to declare war on the United States, an action that would become a significantly important turning point in the way World War II would evolve.

Yoav J. Tenembaum

The German declaration of war against the United States on Dec. 11, 1941, four days after the Japanese attack on Pearl Harbor, on Dec. 7, 1941, was a turning point in the history of World War II, and thus in the history of international relations.

The Japanese attack, which caught the United States by surprise, led to the death of 2,403 people and to a declaration of war by the United States against Japan. The subsequent declaration of war by Germany against the United States introduced the latter into the European theatre, alongside Britain and the Soviet Union. It thus transformed the war in Europe.

Why would Adolf Hitler declare war on the United States when Germany was dealing with a major challenge on its eastern front in the war against the Soviet Union? Why would Germany, on its own initiative, enlarge the war in Europe in such a way as to render it considerably more difficult to win it?

Certainly, Germany had seen the United States not as a neutral power, but rather as pro-British. As far as Germany was concerned, the declaration of war might actually afford it more leeway, more freedom of maneuver to deal with the perceived danger of U.S. military assistance to Britain. Further, Germany asserted that its declaration of war was prompted by its commitment to Japan that it would come to its aid in case of war. However, Germany had promised that it would come to the aid of Japan in case the latter was attacked, which clearly was not the case.

Whatever the reasons that prompted the German declaration of war against the United States, the result was a significant change for the worse for Germany, and a considerable sigh of relief for Britain and the Soviet Union. No matter how much President Franklin Roosevelt wanted to help Britain in the war, he had to deal with a Congress and public opinion wary of foreign entanglements. The Japanese attack, and the subsequent German declaration of war, rallied the country behind the president in fighting a war, which now seemed to be inevitable. The entry of the United States in the war was a turning point as it introduced the most powerful industrial country on earth on the side of Britain and the Soviet Union. Without having to resort too much to counterfactual history, there is little doubt that without the United States, the European war would have developed differently. Britain and the Soviet Union might have won the war, after all, but the price would have been considerably higher and it would have taken significantly more time. Without the United States, the European war might have finished in a stalemate, without a clear winner. What is clear is that the German declaration of war against the United States altered German fortunes considerably for the worse.

To be sure, the United States had been assisting Britain prior to the German declaration of war. However, there was a major difference between assisting Britain and intervening directly on the side of Britain. The full might of the United States was to be deployed against Germany, altering the nature of the war in Europe. Hitler might have thought that by declaring war on the United States he would divide the latter's attention and power between two war theatres and thus weaken it. However, the declaration of war against the United States also led to the weakening of Germany, which had to confront not only the Soviet Union and Britain but also the United States. Hitler apparently believed that, sooner or later, Germany would have had to fight the United States, so maybe it was better to take the initiative and do so sooner when the United States was perhaps not yet prepared for the challenge.

The Japanese attack on the United States enlarged the war significantly by introducing the full might of the latter to the war in the Far East. The declaration of war by Germany against the United States was to the western front in Europe what the German invasion of the Soviet Union was to the eastern front. By its own volition, Germany introduced into the war the two potentially most powerful enemies: the Soviet Union, by launching a surprise attack against it, in June 1941 and the United States, by declaring war against it in the wake of the Japanese attack in Pearl Harbor, in December 1941.

Both actions undertaken by Germany were to become watersheds. However, if Germany might have been able to withstand a war against Britain and the Soviet Union, then the entry of the United States would tilt the balance significantly to the detriment of Germany and its allies. With the benefit of hindsight, the declaration of war by Germany against the United States could be said to have been, in the long run, a crucial turning point as it would render the German war effort in Europe considerably more difficult, if not altogether impossible. In this context, it's interesting to note that the two surprise attacks, by Germany against the Soviet Union, and by Japan against the United States, represented a singularly traumatic experience for the Soviet Union and the United States, respectively, from which both were able to come out ultimately victorious, albeit after a long and bloody war.

For a country veering between isolation by Congress and intervention by the White House, the dilemma of whether to help Britain or not and to what extent, came to a definite end by the Japanese attack on Pearl Harbor and the German declaration of war. The latter was either an act of loyalty or folly. Either Germany wished to display its unflinching support to its Japanese ally, even when it was not obliged to do so, or it sought to demonstrate its self-confidence, following a series of rapid victories in Europe. Nazi Germany had no sense of limits. That led it to invade the Soviet Union and to declare war on the United States, an action that would become a significantly important turning point in the way World War II would evolve.

Originally published in The National Interest, November 21, 2021

Art's Historical License in Netflix's "The Edge of War"

The Netflix movie "The Edge of War" dwells on the international crisis over the Sudetenland in September 1938 and the Munich Conference that settled it, which averted the outbreak of war; a war that would finally break out a year later.

As an artistic production, the movie is undoubtedly good. A captivating imaginary plot takes place as part of a real historical event. The actors are good, and, something which enhances its credibility, those playing the parts of German individuals speak in German and those playing the parts of British individuals speak in English, except in cases in which the same person is able to speak both languages fluently.

Britain's Prime Minister, Neville Chamberlain, is played masterfully by Jeremy Irons. The problem is that he is portrayed as a nice chap with an affable personality, whereas historical evidence shows that he was actually vain, aloof and far from friendly.

Chamberlain is said to have been horrified by the thought of another European war, following the Great War of 1914–1918, which was true. He is portrayed as believing that the next European war would be significantly more destructive than the Great War.

Chamberlain turned out to be right about that, of course.

At the end of the movie, one is told as a fact that, thanks to the year gained by Chamberlain's appeasement policy, and the Munich Agreement, Britain was better prepared to confront Nazi Germany in 1939, and thus win the war.

However, that is not a fact, but an opinion.

By the same token, one could argue that, as a result of Chamberlain's appeasement policy, Germany also gained a precious year to rearm and be better prepared for war, and that, having absorbed the Sudetenland, and subsequently the remainder of Czechoslovakia in March 1939, Germany was able to make use of that country's industrial base and advanced military industry when the Second World War broke out in September, 1939. Indeed, Chamberlain's appeasement policy could be said to have divested the anti-German coalition of a valuable ally, Czechoslovakia, which had a strong army. Strategically, Germany was in considerably better position to initiate hostilities in 1939 than it would have been in 1938. Abandoning Czechoslovakia was not only morally wrong, but also strategically unwise.

It should be stressed that, based on the evidence available, Chamberlain did not seek to postpone war. He attempted to avoid it altogether. He believed that the conflict with Nazi Germany – and, indeed, with Fascist Italy and Imperial Japan – could be settled.

His premise was that Germany's aim was to rectify the wrongs done to Germany by the Versailles settlement at the end of the Great War. The objectives of Germany could be accommodated by a conciliatory disposition and a pro-active diplomacy.

Chamberlain's objective in signing the Munich Agreement was not to gain a year at the expense of Czechoslovakia, the only parliamentary democracy in Central and Eastern Europe. His aim was to solve the conflict with Nazi Germany, not to postpone the outbreak of war. The resolution of the Sudeten Crisis was considered by Chamberlain to be only a step in resolving the overall conflict with Nazi Germany.

Chamberlain believed, as he wrote to one of his sisters, that he was the only person who could settle the conflict with Nazi Germany. His lack of modesty was matched by his ambitious goals. The problem, as it turned out, were not his goals, but rather the premise behind them. After the first meeting with Hitler at Berchtesgaden (Chamberlain would meet him on three different occasions) on the 15th and 16th of September, 1938, Chamberlain wrote to his sister that Hitler "was a man who could be relied upon when he had given his word."

Following the Munich Agreement of the 30th of September, 1938, which had brought to an end the Sudetenland Crisis, Chamberlain suggested to Hitler to sign a piece of paper in which both leaders would pledge that their respective countries would settle all future conflicts by peaceful means, promising never to go to war with each other.

Chamberlain proudly waved that piece of paper in front of all the journalists who were waiting for him at the airport upon his return from Germany.

He announced to the British people that he had brought "peace in our time," hardly the statement of someone who wished to lower expectations, wishing merely to postpone war.

On the same day the Munich Agreement was signed, Chamberlain declared that "the settlement of the Czechoslovak problem which has now been achieved is, in my view, only a prelude to a larger settlement in which all of Europe may find peace."

This is not exactly the mode of conduct and the rhetoric of a leader who sought to postpone war. Rather, it confirms that Chamberlain's objective was to attain an overall resolution of the conflict with Germany – and with Italy. The solution of the Sudetenland Crisis was only a step towards that goal.

Indeed, on the 31st of October, 1938, Chamberlain told his Cabinet that his policy remained "appeasement", the chief aim of which was "establishing relations with the Dictator Powers which will lead to a settlement in Europe and to a sense of stability."

Following the Munich Agreement, Chamberlain argued that he had not sacrificed Czechoslovakia, the only parliamentary democracy in Central and Eastern

Europe. In the House of Commons on the 3rd of October, 1938, Chamberlain explained that the Munich Agreement "may perhaps enable her [Czechoslovakia] to enjoy in the future and develop a national existence under a neutrality and security comparable to that which we see in Switzerland today." As an experienced politician, Chamberlain must have known that his words would be kept on record and come to haunt him if the aim of his policy was merely to postpone war. In the wake of the Munich Agreement, Czechoslovakia resembled anything but Switzerland. Indeed, within a few months it would cease to exist as a separate country following the German invasion of March 1939.

In his declaration of war on the 3rd of September, 1939, which was broadcast on the BBC to the nation, Chamberlain candidly said "You can imagine what a bitter blow it is to me that all my long struggle to win peace has failed." There was no need to refer to his "struggle to win peace" had he been intent on postponing rather than avoiding war. After all, if his aim was merely to postpone war, notwithstanding the sorrow for the war just declared, Chamberlain might have been relieved that, at least, he had managed to gain some precious time before war broke out.

Chamberlain's right-hand man, his closest adviser, Sir Horace Wilson, confirmed many years later that the Policy of Appeasement "was never designed just to postpone war, or unable us to enter war more united. The aim of our appeasement was to avoid war altogether." What is particularly interesting is that, with the benefit of hindsight, he could have tried to enhance Chamberlain's place in the historical record by contending that Chamberlain's objective was more short-term, pragmatic in nature, and less naïve in hindsight. He didn't. Perhaps Sir Horace knew that the evidence available would not allow him to argue otherwise.

To be sure, Chamberlain might have had good reasons to try and postpone war as the movie seems to imply. However, that by itself is hardly a proof that Chamberlain's appeasement policy was designed to postpone war, nor, for that matter, that the year gained consequently led to Britain's victory in the Second World War. Intentions should not necessarily be inferred from results, as the movie attempts to do.

Originally published in History News Network, February 6, 2022

The Death of Appeasement: the 80th Anniversary of the Invasion of Prague

A turning point in the history of international relations refers to an event that alters significantly the present process in international relations, which entails a long-lasting, considerable effect in it. A turning point may not necessarily be the trigger to a significant change in international relations, but rather part of the underlying cause leading to it.

The turning point in the history of international relations in the 1930s occurred in 1939. However, rather than the outbreak of World War II, in September of that year, it was the invasion of German troops to what remained of Czechoslovakia in March 1939, following the Munich Agreement of 1938, that represented that turning point.

It was a significant landmark as it showed even to the most enthusiast supporters of the appeasement policy towards Nazi Germany that German ambitions went much beyond the supposed rectification of the wrongs done to Germany by the Versailles settlement of 1919, following World War I (or the Great War as it was then known).

The appeasement policy pursued by Britain and France was founded on the premise that Germany was maltreated by the victors of World War I, and that

German grievances had some justification and could be accommodated in order to prevent the outbreak of a major European war.

Employing the rhetoric of the parliamentary democracies, Adolf Hitler and the Nazi regime argued that the German people had the right to collective self-determination. Consequently, the prohibition included in the Versailles settlement according to which Austria should remain a separate state and not be allowed to be part of a larger German state was deemed to be unjust. After all, shouldn't the Austrian people 'freely' decide whether they wish to live in a separate sovereign entity or be incorporated into Germany?

By the same token, and following the same logic, Germany argued that the German inhabitants of the Sudeten region in Czechoslovakia should have the right of self-determination. The fact that the area concerned was an integral part of the sovereign territory of Czechoslovakia (incidentally the only truly parliamentary democracy in Central and Eastern Europe) only enhanced the case put forward by Germany. The German population in the Sudeten region was being treated harshly by the government in Prague, claimed Hitler and the Nazi propaganda machine.

Thus, the case for national self-determination was no less valid as regards the German minority in Czechoslovakia than it was in the case of Austria.

The more Germany accused Czechoslovakia for the supposedly inhuman treatment of its Germany inhabitants, the more likely the prospect of a general European war was feared by Britain and France. Why risk such a war if applying the right of collective self-determination could actually avert it?

Of course, Britain's Prime Minister, Neville Chamberlain, thought of that conflict as "a quarrel in a far-away country between people of whom we know nothing." He didn't seem to be particularly concerned with the fate of the German minority in Czechoslovakia or, indeed, with their right of self-determination. His policy, though, was based on the assumption that German grievances in this matter were related to the supposed wrongs inflicted on Germany and the German people following World War I.

To be sure, the real issue was not the quarrel to which Chamberlain referred to, but rather the ambitions of the Nazi regime. After all, even Chamberlain himself asked Hitler whether he had any further territorial demands, beyond the Sudeten region; to which the German leader replied in the negative. Indeed, Hitler stressed cynically, albeit in a rhetorical way, that he was not interested in adding Czechs and Slovaks to the German Reich.

Once German troops entered Prague in March 1939, the whole conceptual edifice justifying German demands collapsed. There was no way anyone could logically justify the German move by resorting to the supposed evils imposed upon Germany by the Versailles settlement. The cherished principle of collective self-determination could apply now in reverse: it was the Czech people who were denied their right of self-determination.

In a sense, it could be argued that the day German forces occupied Prague was the day that the anti-appeasers in Britain, led by Winston Churchill, turned from a cornered minority into a solid majority. It was also the watershed that altered once and for all the character of international relations in Europe: the time for pretense was over. The sense of remorse over the post-World War I settlement and the widely-acceptable principle of national self-determination could no longer justify any policy aimed at preventing war with Nazi Germany.

March 1939 was the real turning point. September 1939 was to be the climax.

Originally published in History News Network, March 17, 2019

Eighty Years Ago, Winston Churchill Became Prime Minister

A landmark day in British and world history.

Yoav J. Tenembaum

On May 10, 80 years ago, Winston Churchill became prime minister of Britain. Germany had already become the dominant power in continental Europe. Within a month and 12 days, France would surrender to Germany. Britain would be left alone to face the full might of Nazi Germany, by then perceived to be invincible. A combination of circumstances and chance would lead Churchill to be chosen as Neville Chamberlain's successor, following the latter's resignation.

A political rival within his own party during the momentous 1930s, three-time Prime Minister Stanley Baldwin, once said that Churchill would make an ideal wartime premier. He turned out to be right.

In a sense, that day in 1940 was a landmark in British and world history. The previous policy of appeasement had failed; Britain was now headed by a leader who had warned about the consequences and was prepared to deal with its repercussions.

Chamberlain truly believed that appeasing Nazi Germany would secure a lasting and stable peace. The premise of his policy was wrong. The means he resorted to in order to achieve his objective was both morally questionable and pragmatically unwise. He thought that by abandoning Czechoslovakia, the only parliamentary democracy in Central and Eastern Europe, he would satisfy the territorial and political ambitions of Nazi Germany. He failed to grasp the true nature of Adolf Hitler's policies and ignored the potential deterrent power of a combined triple alliance of Britain, France, and Czechoslovakia. His suspicion of the Soviet Union (well-founded, to be sure) did not allow him to distinguish between different levels of dangers to the European balance of power.

There was nothing inevitable about Churchill becoming prime minister after Chamberlain, or defiance being chosen as a national strategy.

The policy pursued by Britain up until the full invasion of what remained of Czechoslovakia in March 1939, was premised on the belief that so long as Hitler demanded territories inhabited by German-speaking people, under the guise of the right of national self-determination, Britain could acquiesce. There was this caveat: Germany must attain its objectives by peaceful means. This entailed a logical paradox. If Britain was not prepared to oppose Germany's demands, why would it need to resort to force?

Adolf Hitler's diplomacy was a combination of violent threats aimed at intimidation and empty promises designed to assuage. He found in Chamberlain a partner, ready to accept through proactive diplomacy what his predecessors were prepared to yield passively.

Chamberlain's appeasement was wrong, Churchill maintained, because Hitler didn't merely want to redress the supposed wrongs done to Germany after World War I in the Versailles Settlement. Churchill, whose arguments were steeped in a mixture of moral postulates and pragmatic reasoning, feared that Nazi Germany's ultimate goal was not to alter, but rather to destroy, the prevailing international order. Nazi Germany was thus a threat to be challenged, not an adversary to be pacified.

There was something tragic and yet uplifting as Churchill became premier eight decades ago. His country faced an existential threat. He managed politically to neutralize those within the British political system who advocated a negotiated settlement with Germany aimed at saving Britain from destruction while inspiring an entire nation to stand up alone to it when the odds looked grim.

To be sure, Churchill was not gambling with his country's fate, for he believed that there was no alternative. A negotiated settlement would not be honored by Germany. The only alternative to defiance was surrender. Between the two, Churchill opted for defiance. His singular leadership, his imaginative rhetoric, and the patriotic fervor of the British people ultimately prevailed. Certainly, geography helped. Being an island afforded Britain a margin of security lacking in its continental allies and friends.

Churchill demonstrated that an individual can shape history. There was nothing inevitable about Churchill becoming prime minister after Chamberlain or defiance being chosen as a national strategy. After all, Lord Halifax, who had served as Foreign Secretary under Chamberlain, could have become prime minister. Had he assumed power rather than Churchill, the option of a negotiated settlement might have been pursued, leading perhaps to an entirely different historical scenario.

Winston Churchill had been in the political wilderness for a decade, holding no political office until September 1939, when Chamberlain had appointed him First Lord of the Admiralty. With his deep sense of history, he assessed the present within a larger historical framework. He believed in the old-fashioned concept of the balance of power, traditionally embraced by Britain, whereby no country could be allowed to dominate Europe. He also had faith in parliamentary democracy and alliances based not only on shared interests but also on common values.

Perspectives can change. If Churchill had died in 1929, the year he left government, he might have been remembered as a failed politician; had he died in 1939, the year World War II started, he might have been considered in retrospect as a prophet of doom, who turned out to be right. Because 80 years ago he was chosen to replace Chamberlain as prime minister, we recall him – and quite rightly so – as one of the greatest leaders in modern history.

Originally published in The American Spectator, May 9, 2020

The Last Romantic Zionist Gentile

Referring to the years prior to the creation of the Jewish state, the historian Bernard Wasserstein argues that "No British statesman had a more consistent and more emphatic record of support for Zionism as a solution to the Jewish problem than Winston Churchill." Churchill considered the establishment of the State of Israel "as one of the most hopeful and encouraging adventures of the 20th century." Only eight months subsequent to the proclamation of the State, Churchill suggested to the House of Commons that "The coming into being of a Jewish State in Palestine is an event in world history to be viewed in the perspective not of a generation or a century, but in the perspective of a thousand, two thousand or even three thousand years."

Churchill used to trace his Zionism back to the days of the Balfour declaration, describing himself as "an old Zionist." His attitude toward Zionism remained as passionate and as explicit following his return to Ten Downing Street in 1951. Now, however, with the State of Israel firmly in place, the images he entertained became perhaps more vivid, more colorful, and as ever imbued with historical resonance.

Thus, in June 1954, Churchill stated to journalists

in the United States, "I am a Zionist, let me make that clear. I was one of the original ones after the Balfour Declaration and I have worked faithfully for it." This was merely the introduction. He went on: "I think it is a most wonderful thing that this community should have established itself so effectively, turning the desert into fertile gardens and thriving townships, and should have afforded refuge to millions of their co-religionists who suffered persecution so fearfully under Hitler, and not only under Hitler. I think it is a wonderful thing." In a conversation with Israel's Ambassador in London, Eliyahu Elath, Churchill referred to Israel's population as "the sons of the prophets dwelling in Zion."

Churchill's attitude toward Zionism and the State of Israel was distinctively positive, the images he entertained bordering on the romantic. In this respect, Churchill had no equal among British politicians and officials in the first half of the 1950s. On almost any question pertaining to the country, Churchill's rhetoric, more than that of any other decision-maker or official, was distinctively pro-Israel, reflecting, beyond political considerations and a pure judgement of principle, an emotional attachment to that country and the case it presented.

Thus, on the Suez Canal blockade by Egypt against Israel in 1956, Churchill made it clear to the Foreign Office that "I do not mind it being known here or in Cairo that I am on the side of Israel and her ill-treatment by the Egyptians." On the fate of Jerusalem, Churchill urged Evelyn Shuckburgh, Assistant Under-Secretary at the Foreign Office, "You ought to let the Jews have Jerusalem; it is they who made it famous".

While still Prime Minister, Churchill argued that there was no better army in the Middle East than the Israeli Defence Force, and wished to rely on Israel rather than the Arab states in setting up a regional system of defence against the Soviet Union. He insisted that Israel should be supplied with more jet aircraft than either the defence establishment or the Foreign Office wished. He went on to stress his point by telling his Foreign Secretary, Anthony Eden, "To me the greatest issue in this part of the world is not deserting Israel." In this context, he warned Eden against following in the footsteps of one of his predecessors. "Ernest Bevin, being temperamentally anti-semitic, made the first mistake of backing Egypt against Israel....I hope...that we both equally condemn the Bevinite anti-semitic policy."

More remarkable still, Churchill was in favour of Israel's joining the British Commonwealth. "Do not put that out of your mind," he said to Shuckburgh. "It would be a wonderful thing. So many people want to leave us; it might be the turning of the tide."

Churchill's was Israel's best friend, and as a friend his attitude was shaped by sentiment as much as by pragmatic considerations. He was emotionally attached to Israel and its people, and his stance was a corollary of this. His oft-repeated, self-declared Zionist sympathies, his emotional attachment to the Jewish people and their restored sovereign entity, permeated his attitude toward Arab-Israeli disputes. He was, perhaps the last romantic Zionist Gentile. Or the last romantic Zionist.

Originally published in the Jewish Post of New York, 1996, and reprinted with permission by Finest Hour 102, International Churchill Society, October 5, 2013

The Myth that Hobbles Our Understanding
of the Six Day War

The Six Day War, which took place this month fifty years ago, has left a most enduring legacy. It has convinced the Arab leaders that Israel cannot be destroyed by military means. In a sense, if the Yom Kippur War of October 1973 has led the Arab world to recognize that it should gradually engage in some form of a peace process with Israel, it was the Six Day War of June 1967 that led it to the conclusion that Israel, as a sovereign state, cannot be destroyed militarily.

It is in vogue, particularly in Israel, to recall the Six Day War for the burden it has left the country with, which has had to cope with the occupation of the West Bank and Gaza with its large Palestinian Arab population.

To be sure, a rather ahistorical approach has emerged in this respect. The term "fifty years of occupation" is uttered in a facile manner in reference to Israel's control of the West Bank and Gaza, without paying much attention to the historical complexities which render this term inaccurate.

To begin with, the Oslo Accord signed by Israel and the Palestinian Liberation Organization (PLO) in September 1993, has led to the evacuation by Israel's armed forces of the major centers of population in the West Bank and Gaza and to the establishment of the Palestinian Authority, thus ending Israel's presence in the cities and towns inhabited by Palestinian Arabs that had existed until then.

Certainly, following a spate of terrorist attacks, which led to hundreds of Israeli civilian casualties, in the so-called Second Intifida, the Israeli army launched a military operation in the West Bank in 2002 aimed at destroying the terrorist infrastructure there. Thus, the Israeli armed forces *returned* to the populated areas of the West Bank. Even Saeb Erekat, the chief negotiator of the Palestinian Authority, said then that Israel had *re-occupied* the West Bank. This clearly denotes that, previous to the Israeli military operation in 2002, there had been no Israeli occupation in those areas of the West Bank – as a result of the Oslo Accord.

Also, as far as Gaza is concerned, Israel had evacuated its military forces from the areas inhabited by the Palestinian Arab population as a result of the Oslo Accord of 1993. In 2005, Israel withdrew unilaterally from the entire Gaza Strip, leaving no Israeli soldier or civilian there.

Considering the aforementioned, the phrase "fifty years of occupation" is too categorical and simplistic a statement to be accepted at face value.

Of course, there is an implied criticism of Israeli policy in this regard as if those "fifty years of occupation" could have been ended by an Israeli decision. In this context, there is a tendency to draw a facile comparison between Israel's control of the West Bank and Gaza and colonial rule by European powers up until the second half of the 20th century. According to this line of thought, as the end of colonial rule brought about a solution of the prevailing conflict between the colonial power and the local population so would the end of Israel's control of the West Bank and Gaza produce a solution to the Arab-Israeli conflict and bring about peace and stability to the region.

The differences between the two cases are obvious: A withdrawal from a colony did not constitute a danger to the sovereign territory of the colonial power as the forces fighting for independence did not covet the territory of the colonial power itself. In Israel's case, at least some important segments of the Palestinian leadership, such as Hamas, for example, would not accept any settlement that did not entail the disappearance of Israel as a sovereign state. Even those who claim they would accept a two-state solution, call for the so-called right of return, which, if implemented, might lead to the peaceful destruction of Israel as a Jewish state.

Also, the geographical distance existing between the colonial power and the colony it controlled afforded the first a margin of error which does not apply in Israel's case as the West Bank and Gaza are immediately adjacent to Israel's populated areas. Further, contrary to all major colonial powers in modern history, Israel has to contend with other forces seeking its destruction, which have to be taken into consideration in shaping its national security policy.

A mere mathematical-like formula such as *Israeli withdrawal leads to peace which leads to stability* is thus an oversimplification. That is surely something we can learn from the history of the Arab-Israeli conflict in the last fifty years.

This leads us to an additional observation: However important it is in a historical context, the Six Day War is not the cause, but only an important manifestation of the Arab-Israeli conflict. The Six Day War altered some significant aspects of that conflict. In a sense, it became a watershed as it led to a growing awareness among the Arabs that Israel would not be erased from the map by an act of military will.

Paradoxically, it also sharpened the sense of a distinct, separate Palestinian Arab national consciousness.

Still, many central historical events of the Arab-Israeli conflict occurred *prior* to the Six Day War, such as the founding of the State of Israel, the War of 1947–1949, the 1956 War, the creation in the 1950s of the Palestinian Arab Fedayeen, and of the PLO in 1964, etc. The Arab-Israeli conflict did not start with the capture of the West Bank and the Gaza strip by Israel in June 1967.

Starting the history of the Arab-Israeli conflict in June 1967 is akin to starting the history of the Indian-Pakistan conflict in December 1971.

A landmark in the history of an international conflict, as the Six Day War undoubtedly was, is a particularly significant stage in an already-existing conflict, not its inception.

Originally published in History News Network, June 25 2017

Fifty Years after President Nixon's Visit to China

Few events in modern diplomatic history have astounded
the world as much as Nixon's visit to China.

Yoav J. Tenembaum

Fifty years ago this week, U.S. president Richard Nixon paid an official visit to China, thus ending an official diplomatic boycott that had lasted since the Communists took power in 1949.

The visit, which took place from February 21–28, 1972, was a diplomatic spectacle as few others have been. Few events in modern diplomatic history have astounded the world as much as Nixon's visit to China. Only Egyptian president Anwar Sadat's official visit to Israel in November 1977, which ended the diplomatic boycott of Israel that existed since its foundation in 1948, can be compared to it. Nixon's visit was the culmination of a major diplomatic breakthrough and the beginning of an emerging relationship between the two former foes.

Nixon's visit came in the wake of a secret meeting between U.S. national security advisor Henry Kissinger and China's Prime Minister, Zhou Enlai, in July 1971.

Since the Chinese Communists came to power in 1949, the United States had no official diplomatic contacts with the government in Beijing as it recognized the nationalist government in Taipei, Taiwan, as the legitimate Chinese government.

The enmity between the United States and Communist China reached a peak during the Korean War (1950–1953), when the two countries fought each other.

But increasing hostility between the two Communist powers, the Soviet Union and China, which then led to armed clashes between the two in the winter of 1969, offered an opportunity for the United States to attempt a rapprochement with its long-time rival.

To be sure, before he was even elected president, Nixon had written a *Foreign Affairs* article in 1967 arguing that Communist China was too important to be relegated on the sidelines of the international system.

After becoming president, Nixon and Kissinger set out to explore the possibility of a diplomatic thaw with Communist China. Following some unsuccessful attempts, the Pakistani government, which maintained close links with both countries, facilitated negotiations, finally leading to Kissinger's secret mission to China and subsequently to Nixon's official visit.

An official presidential visit of such a long duration would be difficult to countenance nowadays, particularly with a country with which the United

States has no diplomatic relations. Nixon would describe his visit as "the week that changed the world," which reflected the contemporary view that the visit was a singular turning point in the history of international relations. The same can be said fifty years later.

Following Nixon's visit, the United States had to maneuver between its desire for an ever-closer dialogue with Communist China and its pledge to Taiwan's security. The dilemma facing the United States was not simple. To achieve a rapprochement with Communist China was one thing; establishing full diplomatic relations was another. The United States had to strike a delicate balance between its moral commitment to Taiwan and its pragmatic interest in forging closer links with Communist China. That lead to diplomatic ambiguity, such as the Shanghai Communique published at the end of Nixon's official visit to China, in which the United States stated that "all Chinese on either side of the Taiwan Strait maintain that there is but one China."

This statement, in principle, was something both Communist China and Taiwan could agree on. After all, both believed that there was but one China; they just differed on which regime should rule over it.

Nixon's visit changed the nature of the Cold War. Pursuing a policy of détente towards the Soviet Union, the United States was able to manoeuver between the two Communist powers. Détente created a situation, as Kissinger put it, in which the Soviet Union and Communist China were more distanced from each other than either was from the United States.

Arguably, the bipolar international system that existed until then turned into a tri-polar one.

To be sure, Communist China under Chairman Mao Zedong was a totalitarian state. Mao and his regime were responsible for the deaths of millions of Chinese citizens and the persecution, humiliation, and torture of a large section of the population. The cult of personality in China reached Stalinist levels. The diplomatic opening to Communist China and the long-term effects were certainly not prompted by any ideological affinity.

Indeed, Nixon and Kissinger had already made clear that the principal motivating factor in their foreign policy was serving the U.S. national interest. There was a strong pragmatic streak behind their policy. Ideological reasoning was not completely absent from their decision-making process, but it was secondary. As Kissinger himself would argue many years subsequently, Nixon's rhetoric was more idealistic than his actions; his objectives were defined in Wilsonian terms, while the tactics he employed were more pragmatic.

Nixon did not consider Communist China more politically enlightened than the Soviet Union. Most did not regard Mao and the Chinese Communist leadership as more open-minded than their Soviet counterparts. In this regard, the initiative behind U.S. policy was founded upon a strong belief that Communist China was too important an international actor to be left on the sidelines of U.S. foreign policy. In the context of the Cold War and the prevailing bipolar international system, Nixon believed that a rapprochement with Communist China, which was at loggerheads with the Soviet Union and thus more amenable to opening up a serious diplomatic dialogue with the United States, was needed. Such a policy would lead the Soviet Union to be more flexible towards the United States to prevent a further rapprochement with Communist China. The United States would conduct a policy of détente with the Soviet Union aimed at moderating the super-power conflict, which for its part would lead Communist China to welcome an ever-closer dialogue with the United States to prevent an anti-Chinese alliance between the Soviet Union and the United States.

With the benefit of hindsight, many regarded Nixon's opening to China as his most astounding foreign policy success. It was not merely an ephemeral, tactical achievement, but rather a deeply influential, long-lasting crowning of a presidency marred by the Watergate scandal, which brought about Nixon's downfall in August 1974. Although Watergate tarnished his reputation, Nixon managed to make a remarkable comeback into public acclaim as he became an elder statesman, whose opinions on foreign affairs leaders and policymakers frequently sought.

Originally published in The National Interest, February 22, 2022

Why Putin Miscalculated in Ukraine

It is the gap between expectations and reality that produces surprises in international crises. Apparently, the Ukraine Crisis is no exception.

Yoav J. Tenembaum

Surprise is one of the characteristics of international crises.

A surprise can occur due to the lack of sufficient knowledge or to a mistaken interpretation of the available knowledge. Policymakers' frame of mind is particularly important in international crises. Wishful thinking and confirmation bias can play a fateful role in assessing information. Thus, expecting a better outcome than is warranted by the information available or looking for information that confirms an already-held assumption or view can create unfounded expectations leading to unforeseen consequences.

We lack the necessary information in order to know precisely what Russia's president, Vladimir Putin, expected would happen as a result of the crisis he initiated. We certainly do not possess any reliable information to know what he expected would ensue following the invasion of Ukraine.

What we do know is that the intelligence services of the United States and Britain had correctly assessed that Russia was due to invade Ukraine. We do not know whether they knew what Putin expected would occur in the wake of such an invasion.

But even without reliable information concerning Putin's expectations, we can assume from recent reporting and cautious inferences that Putin was surprised by the united, coherent and powerful response by the United States and its allies. Further, he may have also been surprised by the chain reaction from the private sector, encompassing companies and individuals from finance to sports, and from commerce to culture. According to press reports, intelligence services in the United States and Britain have indicated that the Russians are equally surprised by the difficulty the Russian Army is encountering in Ukraine, having expected a rapid and smooth invasion.

The gap between expectation and reality has led to notable surprises in the history of international crises.

When North Korea invaded South Korea in 1950, the U.S. and South Korean leaderships were caught by surprise. In turn, the leaders of North Korea, the Soviet Union, and communist China were equally surprised when U.S. president Harry Truman decided to react militarily to the North Korean invasion. The United States, for its part, was utterly surprised when China then intervened in the war following the crossing of the 38th Parallel and the counter-attack deep into North Korean territory.

A decade later, President John F. Kennedy was

surprised when he was told in 1962 that the Soviet Union had secretly installed nuclear missiles in Cuba. After all, he had warned the Soviet Union that the United States would never agree to the presence of offensive weapons on Cuban soil, and the Soviet Union had given its pledge it would never place such weapons in Cuba. Even the CIA had assessed only a month before the Cuban Missile Crisis that the chances of the Soviet Union installing nuclear weapons in Cuba were very low. When Kennedy announced to the world about the presence of Soviet nuclear missiles in Cuba, the Soviet leadership was caught by surprise, believing up to then that its secret operation in Cuba was totally unknown to the United States.

When Argentina launched an invasion of the Falkland/Malvinas Islands in the South Atlantic in 1982, the British Government was caught by surprise. The Argentinian military junta, which had ordered the invasion, was in turn surprised by Britain's military response and by U.S. support for Britain following the failure of its mediating efforts. The Argentine government's expectation had been that Britain would not react militarily and that the United States would not back Britain in the ensuing crisis.

Without engaging too much in counterfactual history, it might be possible to assume that had the decision-makers concerned in the aforementioned examples expected a different scenario, they might perhaps have acted differently, thus averting surprise.

For instance, would the Soviet and Chinese leaders, Joseph Stalin and Mao Zedong, have agreed to North Korea's invasion of South Korea had they thought that there was a good chance of U.S. military intervention? Would Truman have consented to crossing the 38th Parallel and invading deep into North Korean territory had he believed that the Chinese would intervene in the war?

Would Argentine president Leopoldo Galtieri have ordered the invasion of the Falkland/Malvinas Islands had he assessed that Britain might react militarily while enjoying support from the United States?

The questions posed do not refer to the outcome of those crises, but only to the prior assumptions leading the decision-makers concerned to reach the decisions they did. Even without knowing in advance what the outcome would be, would they have acted in the way they did had the expectations they entertained been different?

This leads us to the current crisis in Ukraine: Would Putin have ordered the invasion of Ukraine had he expected a united, coherent, and powerful reaction by the United States and its allies? Would he have acted the way he did had he assessed that there might be a widespread international backlash against Russia? Would he have escalated the crisis into a full-blown military invasion had he feared a protracted military campaign?

To be sure, President Joe Biden repeatedly warned Russia that its invasion of Ukraine would result in the imposition of "unprecedented" economic sanctions. The Russian leadership was fully apprised of that. The crisis, which had started several weeks prior to the Russian invasion of Ukraine, had already shown to the Russian leadership that the United States and its allies were diplomatically united in their messages. The warning to Russia was clear and coherent. Of course, there may have been a gap between the intention behind the messages to Russia and the interpretation of those messages by the Russian leadership.

Putin may have believed that Biden was bluffing, as the United States did in 1950 when China warned that it would intervene in the Korean War should U.S. forces cross the 38th Parallel. Alternatively, Putin may have thought that Russia would be able to withstand the effects of economic sanctions, predicting a more limited series of sanctions than were actually imposed, as had occurred back in 2014 following the Russian annexation of Crimea. He may have counted on a weaker response by European countries more closely dependent on trade with Russia.

The reaction of the United States and its allies has been unprecedented. The Russian leadership may have assessed, on the basis of what had transpired in recent history, that whichever steps might be taken against Russia, their consequences would be controllable and affect Russia only to a limited extent. After all, leaders and their advisers tend to look at their rival's modus operandi and extrapolate from it into the future. Intelligence analysts at the CIA in 1962 assessed that the chances of the Soviet Union placing nuclear missiles in Cuba were low because it would run counter to the modus operandi of its leadership. Similarly, Putin may have extrapolated into the future from the West's modus operandi. After all, when was the last time that the United States and its allies responded to a perceived challenge by Russia in such a united, coherent, and powerful manner?

Thus, one may infer that Putin was caught by surprise both by the protracted military campaign in Ukraine and by the unprecedented reaction of the United States and its allies.

It is the gap between expectations and reality that produces surprises in international crises. Apparently, the Ukraine Crisis is no exception.

Originally published in The National Interest, March 16, 2022

How Memories of Hiroshima and Nagasaki Constrain the Ukraine Crisis

If the United States could end World War II in the Pacific theater by dropping two nuclear weapons on Hiroshima and Nagasaki, why, in order to end the Russo-Ukrainian War, wouldn't Russia at least *threaten* to use nuclear weapons?

Yoav J. Tenembaum

Kremlin spokesman Dimitri Peskov said a few days ago that Russia would resort to the use of nuclear weapons only in case of a "threat to the existence" of his country, and not as a result of the current conflict in Ukraine.

Whatever Russia's real motives in the current crisis in Ukraine, Peskov's words seem to reflect a truism widely accepted by the international community: Nuclear weapons are aimed at deterring the other side; they are weapons of last resort, to avoid an existential threat.

Having been used already in 1945, their effects are known. In a sense, a decision-maker in 2022 still lives in the shadow of 1945. U.S. president Harry Truman's decision to drop an atomic bomb on Hiroshima on August 6, 1945, and on Nagasaki three days later, on August 9, in order to end the war against Japan, was a singular turning point in the history of international relations.

Fearing the high estimates of U.S. casualties should the war against Japan continue, Truman resolved to employ a hitherto unknown weapon of unprecedented power. Truman was fully aware that the latest attempts to invade Japanese territory had left a significant number of U.S. casualties. In February 1945, the invasion of Iwo Jima had left nearly 30,000 casualties. In April 1945, the United States invaded the island of Okinawa, leaving around 50,000 casualties in one of the most severe battles of the war against Japan. Estimates of an invasion of mainland Japan were around 130,000. The prospect of invading Japan, with the considerable human toll such an operation was expected to entail, led Truman ultimately to decide to employ a hitherto unknown weapon of unprecedented power to end the war.

The attack on Hiroshima killed 66,000 people and injured 69,000 more; the strike on Nagasaki left 39,000 dead and 25,000 injured. Following the latter, Japan finally surrendered. The scenes of utter destruction and the reports of the high number of casualties left an impact that would remain deep-rooted in the consciousness of future generations of decision-makers.

The atomic bombs dropped on Hiroshima and Nagasaki would become a point of reference: any atomic weapon produced from then on would be compared to those used by the United States in Japan; bomb X would thus be described as being

Y times more powerful than the bombs that fell on both Japanese cities. Hiroshima and Nagasaki have also become a clearly defined dividing line between a pre– and a post-atomic period in international relations. Atomic weapons have altered the character of international affairs.

There was no direct military confrontation throughout the Cold War between the United States and the Soviet Union in part due to their respective possession of nuclear arms. The images of the human and material destruction wrought by the use of atomic weapons in Hiroshima and Nagasaki made it abundantly clear to decision-makers on both sides what the consequences might be if considerably more powerful nuclear arms would be employed.

Indeed, international crises between the two superpowers were managed under the threat of mutually assured destruction – which acted as a constraining factor. Take the Cuban Missile Crisis of October 1962, for instance. One of the reasons it ended without an armed confrontation was the fear of an escalation into a nuclear war.

Paradoxically, atomic weapons proved to be a moderating influence in foreign affairs. In a sense, it was similar to what had occurred in the 1930s. At that time, decision-makers, who had lived through the horrors of World War I, feared the consequences of another European war in which significantly more destructive weapons would be used. Likewise, the post-World War II decision-makers, who had witnessed the horrors brought about by the use of atomic weapons in Japan, feared the consequences of the use of considerably more destructive atomic weapons in a future war.

Nuclear deterrence during the Cold War worked because of a combination of prudence and luck. The United States and the Soviet Union were cautious enough not to descend into a nuclear exchange in any international crisis in which they were both involved. However, fortune – or man-made fortune – played its part as well, such as during the Cuban Missile Crisis. Still, as Louis Pasteur said, "Chance favors the prepared mind." In the shadow of Hiroshima and Nagasaki, concerted and purposeful actions taken to avoid a nuclear confrontation have certainly helped reduce our dependency on chance, and helped us be better prepared for it when unforeseen circumstances arose.

Consequently, Peskov's statement indicates that, notwithstanding the scenes of destruction and human suffering in Ukraine, President Vladimir Putin would not cross the nuclear redline and give an order to employ nuclear arms to achieve his aims – whatever they are – in Ukraine. Nevertheless, considering the problematic record of Russian assurances during the Ukraine Crisis, should Peskov's statement be enough to assuage Russia's rivals?

If the United States could end World War II in the Pacific theater by dropping two nuclear weapons on Hiroshima and Nagasaki, why, in order to end the Russo-Ukrainian War, wouldn't Russia at least *threaten* to use nuclear weapons? What if Russia were to resort to nuclear *blackmail*, whether explicitly or implicitly, to end the war?

Certainly, that scenario appears to be far-fetched. The United States had a nuclear monopoly in 1945; Russia does not in 2022. However, Ukraine is not a member of NATO. As we have seen, Russia is less constrained with regard to Ukraine than it might be concerning any NATO member-state. Would NATO react with a nuclear *threat* against Russia in the face of a Russian nuclear *threat* against Ukraine?

To return to Pasteur, chance favors the prepared mind.

Originally published in The National Interest, April 6, 2022

The Korean War at 70

Remembering the outbreak of a conflict that
still echoes today.

Yoav J. Tenembaum

S eventy years ago, the Korean War broke out. On
June 25, 1950, North Korea invaded South Korea,
leading to one of the gravest crises of the Cold War.

For the leaderships of South Korea and the United
States, the North Korean attack constituted a strategic
surprise for which they were totally unprepared. Yet,
within two days, the administration of President
Harry Truman in the United States managed to
mobilize the United Nations Security Council into
adopting two crucial resolutions. The first criticized
the North Korean invasion and called for its armed
forces to withdraw immediately from South Korea;
the second called on members of the United Nations
to lend assistance to South Korea in its efforts to repel
the invasion.

Truman set a clear objective, to liberate South
Korea, and chose what he believed to be the most
appropriate means to achieve it: eliciting international
support as part of a diplomatic campaign aimed at
delineating a legal framework that would legitimize
the use of force. To be sure, apart from defining
a policy and adopting the tools to carry it out, the

Truman administration took advantage of propitious circumstances that rendered its task considerably easier.

The Soviet Union had been boycotting the United Nations Security Council in protest at the refusal of that body to accept Communist China as a member instead of the Nationalist government, now relegated to Taiwan. The absence of the Soviet representative allowed the United States to pass the two aforementioned resolutions without a veto being cast by the Soviet Union.

An international force was created, led by the United States, to help repel the invasion of South Korea. This was to be an international effort, sanctioned by the United Nations. Truman called it "a police action," denoting a legitimate action by an authoritative entity.

Although caught by surprise, the United States had witnessed how communism was on the advance, gradually but surely: The Berlin Crisis of 1948–1949, the communist coup in Czechoslovakia in 1948, the victory of the communist forces led by Mao Zedong in the civil war in China in 1949, and the loss of the U.S. atomic monopoly to the Soviet Union in 1949.

The invasion of South Korea by North Korea was thus perceived by the United States to be both a continuation of a process but also, in a sense, a turning point. Truman compared it to the German remilitarization of the Rhineland in 1936. In other words, the United States should do in 1950 what Britain and France failed to do in 1936, and take decisive action to head off a worse crisis in the future. Communism was thought to be an expansionist ideology led by a powerful Soviet Union.

The Truman administration had already enunciated its policy toward communism in 1947. The "Truman Doctrine" translated into policy the conceptual precepts of the containment policy advocated by U.S. diplomat George Kennan. Believing that the Soviet Union would take advantage of any opportunity to expand politically and territorially, Kennan recommended that the United States deploy the political, economic and propaganda tools at its disposal to prevent it. Contrary to Nazi Germany, the Soviet Union could be contained by a rational policy of deterrence.

The Soviet and Chinese leadership had aided North Korea in its invasion plans, believing that the United States would not react militarily. They were surprised when it did. When the United States and South Korea decided to cross the 38th parallel, the boundary separating North and South Korea, in a bid to unite the two Koreas under a non-communist regime, their surprise turned into anxiety.

To be sure, China warned the United States through various intermediaries that it would intervene in the war as U.S. and South Korean troops were marching further north, toward the Chinese border. In defining his goals, Truman had made clear to his advisers that he wished to liberate South Korea without getting embroiled in a war with the Soviet Union and/or China. However, China's warnings were dismissed by U.S. officials who argued that China was bluffing. The CIA assessed that neither China nor the Soviet Union would intervene directly in the war so as to avoid a total confrontation with the United States.

China intended to deter. The problem with deterrence is that it fails if it is not perceived to be credible.

The United States was yet again caught by surprise. On November 26, 1950, the Chinese army became directly involved in the war as hundreds of thousands of its soldiers crossed the border to repel the U.S. and South Korean attack on North Korea. What Truman least wanted was actually happening. What began as an internationally-sanctioned diplomatic and military endeavor to liberate South Korea turned into a major military confrontation between the United States and China.

China had backed North Korea in its invasion of South Korea, but now needed to defend North Korea from political extinction. Apart from that, North Korea was important also as a buffer against the United States. The Chinese leadership feared that the ultimate objective of the United States was to attack China and topple the communist regime that had been in power since 1949.

That was certainly not Truman's objective. Indeed, when General Douglas MacArthur, who headed the international force in Korea, urged Truman to expand the war by attacking mainland China, he refused. An attack on mainland China might enlarge the war even further, he feared, leading perhaps to the direct intervention also of the Soviet Union. When MacArthur made public his disagreement with Truman, the latter fired him.

This was an act of supreme leadership by Truman, who knew that MacArthur was enormously popular in the United States, and that his decision might not be welcomed by public opinion. However, he strongly believed that an elected president must prevail over a general. The latter could advise, try to persuade a president, but once a decision had been taken by a president, a general could either implement it or resign. Any other option was unacceptable.

Truman wanted to confine the war to the Korean theater. The direct intervention of China was a most unwelcome development, which he hoped to contain without enlarging the war beyond Korea.

The Korean War would last until July 1953. The ceasefire agreement would restore, in general terms, the territorial and political status quo ante that prevailed prior to the outbreak of war in 1950. This raises the question as to whether the decision during the war by the United States and South Korea to cross the 38th parallel was, with the benefit of hindsight, correct or not. Could the war have finished much earlier than it did, and with considerably fewer casualties? Shouldn't the United States and South Korea have deemed the liberation of South Korea as a victory and stopped the war after having achieved it?

The original decision by the United States with regard to the North Korean invasion was understandable and justifiable, in the short run, and wise in the long run, as it conveyed a deterrent message to North Korea and its communist allies, the Soviet Union and China. An implicit red-line had been drawn by the United States conveying its readiness to defend South Korea, which has outlived many a crisis up to the present. In that respect, the Korean War was a turning point.

With the benefit of hindsight, the decision by the North Korean leader, Kim Il Sung, to invade South Korea turned out to be a serious mistake. He could have paid more dearly than he did had it not been for the direct intervention by China. That could have been avoided, to be sure, had the United States and South Korea not crossed the 38th parallel during the war. However, it ought to be stressed: China and North Korea crossed the 38th parallel in their counteroffensive, which was designed to repel the U.S. and South Korean forces from North Korea. In other words, North Korea and China were bent on destroying South Korea as a separate sovereign entity. Whether the decision by the United States and South

Korea to cross the 38th parallel was correct or not should not be assessed from a moral point of view, but rather from a pragmatic perspective. North Korea had started the war, and it could have ended it with the help of its Chinese ally by stopping at the 38th parallel. It didn't. The war lasted until July 1953 not only because the United States and South Korea had resolved to unite both Koreas under a non-communist regime, but also due to the decision of North Korea and China to attempt, once again, to obliterate South Korea, rather than stop the war at the 38th parallel.

Originally published in The Diplomat, June 24, 2020

The Egypt-Israel Peace Treaty at 40

*Sadat was the only Arab leader who truly understood the
collective psychology of the Israeli people.*

Yoav J. Tenembaum

Forty years ago this month, Egypt and Israel
signed a peace treaty in Washington. It was
the first peace treaty signed by Israel with an Arab
country.

Sixteen months after Egyptian President Anwar
Sadat's visit to Jerusalem, the most powerful Arab
state recognized Israel officially, and formally
committed to live in peace with it.

The peace treaty came in the wake of a difficult
diplomatic process which began with secret dealings
between representatives of the two countries, leading
to an astonishing visit to Jerusalem by Sadat, the first
ever formal visit by any Arab leader to Israel.

Sadat was the only Arab leader who truly
understood the collective psychology of the Israeli
people. In the eyes of Israelis, Sadat's visit transformed
the Arab-Israeli conflict from an intractable dispute
into a manageable disagreement.

Sadat himself used to stress, prior to the signing
of the peace agreement, that "90% of the Arab-Israeli
conflict is psychological." He overstated his case,
but that is irrelevant. Sadat was not speaking as an

objective observer. What is important is that he acted as though the conflict was 90% psychological.

Beyond that, Sadat understood the singular importance of public opinion in the decision-making process of a democracy. He realized that by visiting Jerusalem, he would capture the hearts of the people and thus greatly facilitate the achievement of his diplomatic objectives.

He knew that by eliciting an enthusiastic response from Israeli public opinion he would obtain the support of the people of the United States and their Congress. He would then pave the way for Egypt to get the Sinai Peninsula and a more comprehensive settlement, while creating the basis for a special relationship between Egypt and the United States.

Sadat's thinking was as strategic in concept as it was creative in form.

FOLLOWING THE surprise election victory of his Likud Party on May 17, 1977, prime minister Menahem Begin had to contend with an international campaign of vilification describing him as a warmonger, who might lead the whole region to war.

Begin confounded his critics when he decided to appoint former Labor defense minister Moshe Dayan to be his foreign minister. A well-known figure world-wide, Dayan was to grant Begin's government international legitimacy.

From the outset, Begin and Dayan set on exploring the possibility of a thaw with Egypt. A series of diplomatic moves, among them secret meetings held between Dayan and Egyptian officials, led ultimately to Sadat's visit to Jerusalem. Contrary to what critics contended, Begin never said he would not be ready to reach a territorial compromise with Egypt over the Sinai Peninsula. He even spoke in the same vein with regard to Syria and the Golan Heights.

The bone of contention was the future of the West Bank (Judea and Samaria) and the Gaza Strip. Neither Begin nor Dayan favored a territorial compromise over those territories. Dayan, for his part, spoke of a "functional compromise" that would entail neither Arab nor Israeli sovereignty – at least not on an exclusive basis. Thus, contrary to what was expected of him, Begin decided not to extend Israeli sovereignty over the West Bank and the Gaza Strip, as he promised he would before being elected, pending peace negotiations.

Following Sadat's visit to Jerusalem, Begin devised an Israeli peace plan recognizing Egyptian sovereignty over the entire Sinai Peninsula and offering an autonomous entity to the Palestinian Arabs in the West Bank and Gaza. This autonomy was to be bereft of any sovereign authority. As far as Begin was concerned, it was a "functional compromise," as originally advocated by Dayan. The dream of Israeli sovereignty over the West Bank and Gaza was effectively put in deep freeze.

Sadat had always contended that peace between Egypt and Israel, in any case only possible in future generations and not during his lifetime, would not be feasible unless Israel withdrew to the lines of June 4, 1967, on all three fronts (the boundaries prevailing prior to the Six Day War).

THE FINAL peace agreement, based on the Framework for Peace signed at Camp David in September 1978 – with the active mediation of then US president Jimmy Carter – reflected a change of position by both Sadat and Begin.

Egypt agreed to sign a peace treaty with Israel that did not entail a full Israeli withdrawal from all the territories captured during the Six Day War – and the agreement did not wait for future generations of Egyptians to be signed, but was signed by Sadat himself.

As part of his consent to withdraw completely from the Sinai Peninsula, Begin agreed to dismantle the Israeli settlements in the area, something he vowed he would not do. Furthermore, a fully autonomous entity was to be established in the West Bank and Gaza for an interim period of five years, following which negotiations were to be held aimed at determining the final status of the territories concerned.

The negotiations that were held between Egypt and Israel – following the peace agreement, aimed at implementing the autonomy plan for the Palestinian Arabs in the West Bank and Gaza – were discontinued by Sadat, who argued that Israel was not negotiating in earnest.

The peace treaty between Egypt and Israel changed the strategic position of Israel in the area. Egypt was no longer the leader of the warring Arab coalition. Rather, with the years, it became a diplomatic bridge between Israel and the Arab world.

Also, as we have witnessed in recent years, the challenge posed by Iran and its regional allies, as well as by Sunni terrorist groups such as Al Qaeda and Islamic State, has led to a tacit strategic alliance between Israel and the Sunni countries in the Middle East.

Egypt and Israel cooperate in the fight against terrorist forces in the Sinai Peninsula. It is difficult to imagine such cooperation without the peace agreement signed forty years ago by those two countries. Indeed, it could be argued that without that peace agreement, the current tacit alliance between Israel and the Sunni Arab states would have been less likely to emerge in the way it has in recent years.

To be sure, the Egypt-Israel peace agreement is embraced by the security establishment in Egypt, but much less so by the people, particularly the professional elites, who harbor a degree of hatred towards Israel not unlike that which prevailed prior to Sadat's visit to Israel.

Whereas, to begin with, Israelis entertained a romantic image of what peace would look like following a peace agreement with Egypt, with ever closer links between the two people being forged, a more sober attitude prevails now: Israelis seem to be content with the continuation of non-belligerency and regional cooperation against common enemies. This appears to characterize Israeli attitudes to peace in general: security is regarded as paramount; friendship at the popular level can wait.

Perhaps neither Sadat nor Begin imagined peace to look as it does now, forty years later. Their actions, though, altered the strategic environment of the Middle East more significantly than any other diplomatic process in the last seventy years.

Originally published in The Jerusalem Post, March 11, 2019

80 Years Later: The Conference that Led to The Final Solution

The Wannsee Conference translated Hitler's words
into action in the most detailed, coherent and efficient
manner possible.

Yoav J. Tenembaum

The Wannsee Conference of January 20, 1942, called to coordinate the German plan to undertake "The Final Solution to the Jewish Problem," was a turning point in the history of Europe. It put the seal on the first coordinated, organized, industrial plan to eliminate completely an entire nation from the face of the earth.

To be sure, the Nazis and their collaborators throughout Europe had persecuted and killed Jews en masse prior to the Wannsee Conference. From 1933 onward, the Nazi Party, and the German state as a whole, had adopted measures, which increasingly limited the freedom of action of Jews, turning them into individuals bereft of any legal rights. Jews were persecuted, attacked and expelled.

What started in Germany was subsequently applied in Austria, following the Anschluss of March 1938; in the Sudetenland, in the aftermath of the Munich Agreement of September 1938, and extended to what remained of Czechoslovakia after the German occupation in March 1939.

When World War II started in September 1939, with the invasion of Poland by Germany, the Polish Jewish community, the largest in Europe, became immediately a target of German persecution. Around 3 million Jews were trapped under German rule, with scant possibility to leave. The Jews were turned into a ghettoized community, with the fortunate ones barely able to survive, and many starving to death or randomly killed.

Following the German invasion of the Soviet Union in June 1941, Jews were executed, en masse – women, men and children. The killing of thousands upon thousands of Jews by gunfire was taking a toll on German fighting forces in the Soviet Union.

The method was thought to be inefficient, as millions of Jews were to be murdered in the midst of a difficult war: too much time and too many Germans would be needed. Thus emerged the idea of "The Final Solution to the Jewish Problem." A means was sought to eliminate the Jewish people, not by gunfire, but rather by gas; an industrial-like formula that would achieve the goal of killing every Jew in Europe quickly and efficiently.

Europe, which had witnessed 2,000 years of anti-Semitic persecution, reached a peak unequaled in the history of humankind. The Final Solution was put into effect by one of the most cultured nations the world had ever known. The Jewish people were to disappear from the face of the earth in a few years. Nothing would remain of the Jewish nation, no Jew would prevail, nothing but the ashes of the corpses gassed to death would survive.

This plan was as meticulous in preparation as it was to be in implementation. Six million Jews would perish during the Holocaust. Had it not been for the victory of the Allied armies, many more Jews would have perished, perhaps every Jew still alive under German rule.

THE ELIMINATION of the Jews of Europe was to be the corollary of a well thought-out plan, meticulously carried out, and enthusiastically embraced, rather than the by-product of the war. Jews were to disappear not as a result of a series of mass murders, but as an integral part of a coherent, industrial program. For the German leadership, the Final Solution was to be as important an objective as winning the war.

Many people in Europe collaborated with Nazi Germany in persecuting and murdering Jews. Indeed, some proved to be even more enthusiastic in their anti-Jewish fervor than the Nazis. Whether they were Ukrainians, Lithuanians, Poles, Latvians, Hungarians, Romanians, French, Dutch, or anyone else, they displayed a sense of sadism that on occasion surprised the Germans themselves.

Without Nazi Germany, the Holocaust would not have happened, but without their collaborators throughout Europe, it would have been more difficult to carry it out.

In the meeting at Wannsee, representatives of various government agencies participated, such as the Reich Chancellery, the Department of Justice, the Foreign Ministry, the Gestapo, the SS, and the Race and Resettlement Office. The meeting was headed by Reinhard Heydrich, who held various high-ranking official posts, and assisted by Adolf Eichmann, chief of Jewish affairs for the Reich Central Security Office.

The Wannsee Conference was a secret gathering, known only to a handful of German officials. However, the implementation of its decisions depended on many, many more people, who might not have been privy to all the details discussed at that conference. There is no need for a great number of people to devise a plan aimed at eliminating an entire nation, but there is certainly a need for a great number of people to carry it out.

The Wannsee Conference was a turning point, no doubt, but it would be nearly impossible to comprehend it but as part of a process. After all, it was convened in order to make the persecution and murder of Jews, which had been taking place until then, a much more efficient and significantly more rapid operation. It was both a continuation and a clear-cut new beginning.

Adolf Hitler made clear what his intentions were regarding the fate of the Jews in Europe back in January 1939. At a speech before the Reichstag (the German parliament, which by then was a mere institutional figurehead devoid of any powers), Hitler stated that "If the international Jewish financiers in and outside Europe should succeed in plunging the nations once more into a world war, then the result will not be the Bolshevization of the earth, and thus the victory of Jewry, but the annihilation of the Jewish race in Europe!"

The Wannsee Conference translated Hitler's words into action in the most detailed, coherent and efficient manner possible.

Originally published in The Jerusalem Post, January 8, 2022

40 Years since Israeli Attack on Iraq's Nuclear Reactor

The Begin Doctrine ought to be understood in the context of Israel's history and particular circumstances as a small country with no geographic depth, surrounded by enemies bent on its destruction.

Yoav J. Tenembaum

Forty years ago this month, on June 7, 1981, the Israel Air Force launched a surprising and successful attack, known as Operation Opera, against Iraq's nuclear reactor at Osirak. This was to be a turning point in the history of the Middle East as the so-called Begin Doctrine was born, whereby Israel would never allow a hostile country to develop nuclear weapons. Thus, in 2007, Israel launched a surprising and successful attack against Syria's secret nuclear reactor in the Deir ez-Zor region; and for many years, Israel has been conducting both a public and secret campaign aimed at thwarting Iran's nuclear program.

Israel's attack on Iraq's nuclear reactor occurred in the midst of the Iran-Iraq War. Iran had already tried – unsuccessfully – to attack the Osirak nuclear reactor. In spite of this, the Iraqi leadership, led by Saddam Hussein, was taken totally by surprise by Israel's action. This was due to the meticulous Israeli plan, which took a few years to prepare and was carried out in a singularly professional manner.

The Israeli government led by prime minister Menachem Begin had exhausted all diplomatic avenues to thwart Iraq's plans before it reached the conclusion that there was no option but to destroy Iraq's nuclear reactor by force. The decision-making process in Israel was long, thorough and detailed. Begin believed that all options had to be assessed and every opinion heard.

The United States ambassador to Israel, Samuel Lewis, had already conveyed to the State Department long before Israel's attack that Israel was adamant that if diplomacy should lead nowhere, it would ultimately resort to military means to put an end to Iraq's nuclear program. Thus, contrary to what then-US president Ronald Reagan was led to believe immediately after he was apprised of Israel's attack, Israel had warned the US about the consequences of diplomatic failure. The documents concerned were apparently not forwarded by the outgoing administration of president Jimmy Carter to the incoming Reagan administration.

To be sure, Israel was roundly criticized by the international community, including the United States, for its attack. However, the US administration was hardly monolithic on this. Whereas vice president George H.W. Bush, White House chief of staff James Baker, and defense secretary Caspar Weinberger were particularly critical and wanted to sanction Israel, secretary of state Alexander Haig and US ambassador to the United Nations Jeanne Kirkpatrick displayed a more nuanced attitude.

INDEED, ACCORDING to then US national security advisor Richard Allen, Haig had confided to him that he was in two minds about it. On the one hand, he wished to support Israel's action, but on the other, he was pressured by the State Department and governments in the Middle East to come out strongly against it. For her part, Kirkpatrick was known to be in favor of Israel's attack, but had to maneuver within the State Department in order to strike a delicate diplomatic balance. The US delegation to the UN would support a UN Security Council Resolution condemning Israel so long as sanctions against it were not included.

Following the First Gulf War in 1990–1991, many politicians in the US thanked Israel for its 1981 attack against Iraq's nuclear reactor. According to his aides, Haig had already anticipated that the day would come when the United States would thank Israel for what it did.

According to secret records that became available as a result of the Second Gulf War in 2003, Saddam Hussein's intentions had been made crystal clear to his government and military: Israel was an implacable enemy that had to be destroyed. Nuclear weapons were necessary to deter Israel and help the Arab world achieve victory against it in an all-out war. If the Arab armies were to reach the outskirts of the main Israeli cities, Israel, he believed, would threaten to use its own nuclear weapons to avoid destruction. Iraq's nuclear arms would become necessary then in order to deter Israel and attain its objective.

Israel perceived Iraq as a mortal enemy. Its leaders believed that Saddam was a singularly dangerous enemy. Begin spoke openly about his fear of an Iraqi nuclear device being used against Israeli civilians.

The Begin Doctrine ought to be understood in the context of Israel's history and particular circumstances as a small country with no geographic depth, surrounded by enemies bent on its destruction. In fact, Israel is the only country on Earth whose very existence is called into question. As far as Israel is concerned, nuclear deterrence (assuming Israel has nuclear weapons) is not an option against a hostile country like Saddam Hussein's Iraq or the Islamic Republic of Iran.

The other side of the Begin Doctrine, even though it has never been mentioned as such, is that Israel should do its utmost to moderate regional conflicts and achieve peace when possible. Thus, Begin left a two-fold legacy: the attack against Iraq's nuclear reactor and the peace agreement with Egypt.

Originally published in The Jerusalem Post, June 9, 2021

Margaret Thatcher's Achievements

She had core beliefs which she adhered to without compromise

Yoav J. Tenembaum

Margaret Thatcher was a stateswoman in the fullest sense of the word. She had a coherent vision, articulated it in simple (some would say simplistic) terms and implemented it with passion.

She had core beliefs which she adhered to without compromise. Not in vain was she known as the "Iron Lady." However, the legend that she was obdurate all the time on every issue is historically questionable. When deemed necessary, on occasion, she would display a pragmatic streak designed to overcome obstacles on the way to achieving desired ends.

She was the longest-serving British prime minister of the 20th century. She won three consecutive elections and lost only to her cabinet colleagues who failed to support her following the results of the first round of leadership elections with her Conservative Party in 1990. She never lost a general election as prime minister.

When she was first elected prime minister in 1979, Britain was seen as "the sick man of Europe." When she left office in 1990, Britain was regarded as an economically vibrant country and diplomatically influential actor in the world stage. The economic policies adopted by her governments, particularly her first one, led to high unemployment and social divisions, but they also brought a considerable change in the economic system of Britain. The policies of her governments have been emulated by other leaders in other countries. Even New Labour headed by Tony Blair refused to undo most of the reforms instituted by Thatcher and her governments.

Few leaders have lent their names to a whole economic philosophy as Thatcher has. Thatcherism is a by-word for economic policies favoured by some and denigrated by others.

Although staunchly anti-Communist she was the first Western leader to declare that Soviet leader, Michael Gorbachev, was a man she could do business with.

Foreign policy turned out to be a turning point in her political life.

Her political fortune changed significantly in the midst of economic recession for the better following the invasion of Argentina of the Falklands/Malvinas Islands on the 2nd of April, 1982. Her resolute leadership and Britain's military victory led ultimately to a Conservative landslide in the 1983 elections.

Thatcher's resignation as prime minister came in the wake of a serious internal rift in her government over Britain's policies towards Europe.

In both cases, she was trying to be resolute. In the

first, she won; in the latter, she lost.

Thatcher was loyal to those who were loyal to her and scathing to those who were critical or were thought to be critical of her policies. She could be supportive but also offensive.

She was a woman playing politics in a game of men. She had to fight her way up, and her way in, among suspicious men who, on occasion, would denigrate her.

To be sure, as some ministers have acknowledged, she could make use of her femininity in order to pursue her goals. Her stiff public image was a true reflection of her politics, though not always of her personality.

Former French President, Francois Mitterrand, is attributed to have said about her that "she had the eyes of Caligula and the lips of Marilyn Monroe."

Before she became leader of the Conservative Party in 1975, Thatcher said that she didn't believe that a woman would become prime minister in Britain in her life-time.

She was a true friend of the Jewish People and the State of Israel, although she had some serious reservations about Menachem Begin's polices. She admired Jews and Jewish culture.

Thatcher was not a consensus-seeking politician. She was an ideologue who believed that politics should be an arena in which ideas become reality. Interestingly enough, some of the more radical members of the Labour Party during her premiership used to speak in her favour, arguing that what she did for "her class" is exactly what Labour should do for its own.

Originally published in the Jerusalem Post, April 10, 2013

Fifty Years since the Death of Winston Churchill

Churchill was a complex human being.

Yoav J. Tenembaum

Winston Churchill died 50 years ago this year. After having been eulogized as perhaps the greatest leader of the 20th century, it has recently been in vogue to dwell on Churchill's mistakes.

To be sure, there were many. It is also quite common now to refer to some of his more objectionable statements. There were a few of them, too. The famous historian Andrew Roberts, hardly a critical observer of Churchill, does not mince words to describe Churchill's rude and inconsiderate mode of conduct with his professional entourage.

All of the above just makes Winston Churchill a complex human being, which he certainly was. He was not an angel, to say the least. If I had to choose between having a cup of tea with Churchill or with Stanley Baldwin, who served on three different occasions as British prime minister, I would no doubt choose the latter, no matter how less familiar he is to people today.

Let us be candid: If Churchill had died in 1929, the year he left government, he might have been remembered as a failed politician; had he died in

1939, the year World War II started, he might have been considered in retrospect as a prophet of doom who turned out to be right. Because he died in 1965, we recall him – and quite rightly so – as one of the greatest leaders in modern history.

To claim that his record from 1933, the year the Nazi Party came to power, to 1945, the year the Allies won World War II, erases every error he made or any objectionable opinion he held prior to 1933 is as persuasive as claiming, vice versa, that the latter diminishes the singular effect of what he did and said from 1933 to 1945.

Churchill demonstrates that an individual can shape history. This can be shown by merely posing a "what if" question: What would have happened had Lord Halifax, rather than Churchill, been appointed British prime minister following the resignation of Neville Chamberlain in May 1940? After all, Lord Halifax was a strong candidate to replace Chamberlain. It was hardly inevitable that Churchill should have succeeded him.

Based on the information available to us today, we can safely assume that Lord Halifax would have sought a peace agreement with Nazi Germany as Britain was standing alone and fearing for its sovereign existence as an independent state. Churchill refused to follow that path, preferring to continue the fight to the end.

Churchill also demonstrates that rhetoric and leadership can make a difference. His oratory inspired the British people, his leadership guided them, in a period where suffering was rife and victory seemed remote.

Churchill became a symbol, not only for the people he led, but also for all those around the world who prayed for Britain to win.

Baldwin, whom we mentioned above, had said that Churchill could turn out to be an ideal wartime leader.

This speaks well not only of Baldwin's political intuition, but of his personal integrity, for he said so as he was being criticized by Churchill for his policies as prime minister toward Nazi Germany between 1935 and 1937.

His singular achievement as a wartime leader notwithstanding, the Conservative Party led by Churchill lost the 1945 general elections. Churchill, who was distraught, is said to have replied to his wife, trying to console him that this might be a blessing in disguise, that "so far, it is very well-disguised."

He returned to 10 Downing Street following the general elections of October 1951, and would serve as prime minister until April 1955. During his second term as prime minister, Churchill would suffer a stroke. During his second premiership Churchill would try to shape events as he had done during his first, but his health would not allow him to be as effective.

Nevertheless, it was during those years that Churchill became the guardian angel of Israel in

Britain. The documents of that period in British archives demonstrate quite clearly that Churchill saw himself as a Zionist.

He made it abundantly clear to his foreign secretary, Anthony Eden, that Israel was uppermost in his mind.

He urged Eden to support Israel and not emulate what he termed "Bevin's anti-Semitic policies." There was hardly a question pertaining to the Middle East that did not prompt Churchill to defend Israel's position, to guard against those who might harm its interests.

His words on Israel, both in writing and in private conversation, were imbued with an emotional tone which went well beyond pragmatic reasoning.

As leader of the Opposition, Churchill had said that the establishment of the State of Israel was "an event in world history to be viewed in the perspective not of a generation or a century, but in the perspective of a thousand, two thousand or even three thousand years." The same might be said about his own leadership from 1933 to 1945.

Originally published in The Jerusalem Post, February 3, 2015

Richard Nixon, from Mean-Spirited Disgrace to Elder Statesman

R ichard Nixon was a man of contradictions.
He was brilliant at delineating a worldview and mean at describing his fellow human beings. His political thoughts could be all-encompassing in their reach while his personal instincts could be very short-sighted in their horizon. He said his dream was to further the cause of world peace, but he did much to create discord with individuals.

It should be noted, though, that Nixon had close friends and intimate political assistants who were loyal to him.

He did not discriminate. His disdainful comments about minority groups applied to them all without discrimination: Jews, Italians, Poles, African Americans, etc. He could be equally denigrating in his remarks about them all.

On the other hand, he would have no problem whatsoever working with people who belonged to any of those minorities he disliked. Nixon drew a line between his personal dislike of a minority group and the political allegiance of an individual. If a person shared his worldview, Nixon was more than ready to have him on his staff, notwithstanding his ethnic or religious background. The closest person to him in shaping foreign and national security policy was Henry Kissinger, a Jew with whom Nixon, in his twisted ironic manner, would share his anti-Semitic remarks.

His was a peculiar case: he was shy and introvert and yet he was in a world of outgoing and extrovert people, the world of politics.

Nixon popularized and made his own a memorable phrase: "The Silent Majority." Three words that encompass Nixon's genuine belief that a silent majority of the people in the United States backed him; and that the minority that did not was simply more visible and audible. Reality warranted Nixon's phrase, at least until the Watergate affair inundated his presidency. What better phrase for a president who was shy and introvert?

Nixon was the architect of many foreign policy successes. However, as time elapsed, some of them were seen by posterity as less glowing in the distance then they seemed to be at the moment of creation.

To be sure, due to Watergate, he was compelled to be much less involved in preserving the foreign policy processes he had initiated. He built the edifice, but was hardly there to maintain it. How would détente with the Soviet Union have fared had Nixon's mind been free from the Watergate affair? How would the Vietnam debacle have looked like had he stayed on to finish his second term?

The problem was not only that Nixon had to face Watergate and then resignation, but that Congress was hardly in the mood to sustain a weak South Vietnam or actively to confront an expansionist Soviet-led campaign in the Third World.

How absurd can it be that Nixon, who won his re-election in 1972 by a huge margin, should have had around him people who thought it was necessary to do what they did at the Watergate to secure his re-election?

Without the benefit of hindsight, Nixon could have won comfortably in 1972 by just sitting in the White House and waiting patiently for election day to arrive. The seventeenth-century French mathematician and philosopher, Blaise Pascal, once wrote that the world would be a much better place if everyone just sat quietly in his/her own room. Had Nixon and his assistants followed Pascal's dictum during the election campaign in 1972, history might have looked considerably different.

Nixon's tragedy was that he had a statesman's vision within the mental framework of a mean-spirited paranoid. Certainly, he thought he was being persecuted. Indeed, more often than not reality seemed to have proved him right. The problem was that, on many an occasion, his mode of conduct was responsible for that. He helped create the situation, to begin with, about which he subsequently complained.

Well, to be fair to him, his political rivals were not always innocent bystanders. Some of his rivals were hardcore ideologues bent on his political destruction;

some others simply could not stand him. The world of politics produces likes and dislikes that go beyond ideas. Nixon's is a particularly prominent case study of that.

Nixon chose Henry Kissinger to be his national security adviser following his victory in 1968. Kissinger was not part of the inner group of Nixon's assistants and advisers. He ended up, though, being the closest person to Nixon in shaping foreign and national security policy, an area which the president was most interested in and where he had his most striking successes.

Nixon held three summit meetings with the leader of the Soviet Union, an unprecedented feat. He was the first U.S. president to meet a Soviet leader in Moscow and to receive him in the United States.

He was the first U.S. president to sign a comprehensive agreement with the Soviet Union putting a cap on the increase in nuclear weapons held by both superpowers (SALT I).

Nixon was the first president to pay an official visit to Communist China. Following more than twenty years of an official boycott, China was re-incorporated into the realm of U.S. foreign policy. A singular diplomatic achievement, the opening to China was perhaps Nixon's greatest foreign policy success. Kissinger played a central role in the diplomacy that preceded Nixon's achievements in the international arena.

Thus, through the so-called Shuttle Diplomacy conducted by Henry Kissinger in the wake of the Yom Kippur War of 1973, the Nixon administration managed to secure three interim agreements between Israel and its Arab neighbors: two with Egypt and one with Syria.

By then, Kissinger had already been appointed as Secretary of State, in addition to his post as National Security Advisor: the first and only person so far to have held both positions simultaneously in U.S. history.

Nixon and Kissinger shared a common conceptual view of foreign policy, and more than one common personal trait. They were both realists. According to the realist school of international relations, the international system is anarchic, and each country seeks to enhance its power in order to further its national interests. Ideology plays a secondary role, if at all. Similarly, both Kissinger and Nixon were paranoid and bent on secrecy. The diplomacy they conducted was founded upon secrecy and *realpolitik*.

Without the secrecy, the China opening might have failed. However unpalatable to the State Department that felt, rightly, excluded, Kissinger's secret diplomacy bore fruits in reaching the SALT agreement and the peace accord with North Vietnam.

Secrecy in the conduct of diplomacy should be distinguished, in this context, from the results it produces. The agreement ultimately reached must be made public; not necessarily the way to achieve it. The veil of secrecy may be a necessary means to negotiate without outside pressure; making the final agreement public knowledge is essential for it to have legitimacy.

The problem with the Nixon-Kissinger diplomatic style, particularly while Kissinger served as National Security Adviser and not as Secretary of State, was that negotiations were concealed not only from the public, but also from the highest-ranking U.S. diplomats. This created mistrust and frustration in the decision-making system. The result was internal infighting that was played out through leaks and which were ultimately detrimental to all concerned. As President Dwight Eisenhower used to say, when individuals and organizations feel that they are active participants in the decision-making process, the chances of obstruction in the implementation of policy decreases significantly.

Policy was decided upon and mostly conducted by Nixon and Kissinger, which led to an efficient, rapid and coherent process. Indeed, policy was clear and unambiguous; but so was the internal opposition to it. Nonetheless, Nixon found in Kissinger his ideal partner for shaping foreign policy. Kissinger found in Nixon an ideal president to implement his conceptual worldview and to realize his personal ambitions.

Nixon would end his presidency as a seventh-rate politician, but would subsequently end his life as a widely-respected and admired statesman. His comeback was amazing. Time was able to work for him; but so was his fervent desire for recognition. He worked hard to achieve it, to be sure. Doing so outside the political system was paradoxically easier. He was no longer politically active, which helped him build an image of a wise statesman, well above the daily political quarrels.

Like Janus, the Nixon of past days, the mean-spirited politician, the person responsible for obstructing the law, was facing backwards; the Nixon who was resting in peace at his funeral, the brilliant world-statesman, the respected analyst of international affairs, was looking forward.

Like Janus, the two were one and the same. One can hardly think of a more intriguing contradiction in modern history.

Originally published in History News Network, January 19, 2012

Sixty Years of British-Israel Ties

Sir Francis Evans, Britain's first ambassador to Israel, was in a sense Israel's guardian angel.

Yoav J. Tenembaum

Sixty years ago, Sir Francis Evans became Britain's first ambassador to Israel.

During his nearly three years of service in that role, Evans became, in a sense, Israel's guardian angel. When Sir John Troutbeck, Britain's ambassador to Iraq at the time and perhaps the most pro-Arab British envoy in the Middle East, urged the Foreign Office to adopt a much more favorable policy towards the Arab world at the expense of Israel, Evans retorted simply and powerfully. "It would be immoral to for us to abandon Israel in this way," said Evans.

The Balfour Declaration, said Evans, was largely responsible for creating the State of Israel, and so Britain had a moral responsibility toward the new country.

Furthermore, Evans questioned whether an unequivocal pro-Arab policy would not be counter-productive. Might not the Arabs, he asked, perhaps rhetorically, "interpret a withdrawal of our support from Israel as a sign of weakness which they should exploit, rather than an expression of friendship meriting gratitude?" The Foreign Office in London fully concurred with Evans.

To be sure, Evans was not a blind supporter of Israel's policies.

Indeed, he favored trying to achieve peace between Israel and the Arab world by "trying to bring pressure to bear on both sides." However, he was motivated by a moral postulate with regard to Israel. Evans thought that Britain had to keep its obligations, notwithstanding any pragmatic considerations which might indicate an apparent benefit to siding with the Arabs.

Evans was there, so to speak, whenever Israel's basic case was questioned, arguing with a judicious blend of reason and emotion.

He was a professional diplomat, with years of experience.

No less important, he was sensitive in understanding the Israeli side of the argument and sharp in analyzing the undercurrents of the complex regional situation in the early 1950s.

Evans had served for many years as British consul in Boston, New York and Los Angeles. He then served in a senior position at the Foreign Office in London before being sent to Israel at the beginning of 1952, first as Britain's minister and from September 1952 as ambassador, when the legation in Tel Aviv was elevated to the status of embassy.

His first impressions of Israel reflect his poetic streak. Drawing upon his US experience, he compared Israel with the southern part of

California. "The similarities," he claimed, "are largely physical." However, it was in the human domain where he encountered similarities which inspired him to articulate, in exquisitely vivid language, a particularly colorful analogy: "There is here, as in Southern California, the mingling of many races."

He went on to compare the Californians of Spanish stock with the Arabs, the Mexicans and the East Indians with the Yemenites, the conservative settlers of Los Angeles City and its satellites with the commercial and professional German Jews, the driving and optimistic "boosters" of Southern California with the enthusiastic and no less optimistic Russian Zionists of Israel.

"There is throughout both areas," Evans concluded, "a spirit of adventure, of purpose, of determined and hopeful upbuilding, coupled with an intense – perhaps an inordinate – pride of achievement."

On the May 4, 1952, the Israeli Cabinet decided to move the Foreign Ministry from Tel Aviv to Jerusalem. The Israeli Foreign Ministry explained this decision in wholly pragmatic terms. The move was not intended as a political demonstration. It was rather an internal organizational imperative. The permanent separation from other government ministries and from the Knesset affected the work of the ministry, hindering its efficiency.

To begin with, Evans argued before his

government that a delay in the implementation of the decision ought to be secured.

What is interesting is the wording used in this regard: the move to Jerusalem was "premature," stressed Evans. Indeed, when Evans met the director-general of the Israeli Foreign Ministry, Walter Eytan, he conveyed to him that the transfer was considered to be "inopportune."

There appeared to be no opposition in principle to the move on his part; certainly he evinced no desire to argue his case vis-avis the Israeli government from a principled, rather than a pragmatic, position.

Evans suggested to his government that, if there was no general agreement by the three Western powers (US, Britain and France) to object to the proposed move, Britain should prepare to move its legation (later embassy) to Jerusalem.

He argued that if Britain delayed action until the last possible moment, "the Israelis would find our attitude a little unfriendly and very difficult to understand."

Evans made it clear that his suggestion was designed to facilitate the work of the British diplomatic staff with the Israeli government in Jerusalem.

The Foreign Office in London was persuaded by Evans' arguments; indeed, its legal department maintained that moving the British Legation to Jerusalem would be in accordance with international law as long as it was stipulated that such a moved did not entail any legal recognition of Israel's claim of sovereignty over the Western part of the city which it controlled.

The Israeli government waited a year before implementing its decision to move the Foreign Ministry to Jerusalem. By then, circumstances had changed. Had Israel proceeded to carry out its decision sooner, Evans' suggestion might perhaps have become a

reality. He might have thus served not only as the first British ambassador to Israel but also as its first diplomatic envoy to Jerusalem, its capital.

Originally published in The Jerusalem Post, January 14, 2012

Samuel Lewis in Israel, 1977–1985

*Samuel Lewis' ambassadorship in Israel demonstrates
how a professional diplomat can have an important
influence on the shaping of foreign policy.*

Yoav J. Tenembaum

Thirty years ago, the late FSO Samuel W. Lewis
ended an eight-year tenure (1977–1985) as the
United States ambassador to Israel. Besides being
the longest-serving U.S. diplomatic representative to
Israel, he was almost certainly the most popular.

Prior to his appointment, Lewis, a career Foreign
Service officer since 1954, had served in Italy,
Brazil and Washington, D.C. Only his 1975–1977
assignment as head of the Bureau of International
Organization Affairs had given him any firsthand
experience with the Arab-Israeli dispute.

Lewis recalled many years later that he had been
offered the choice of an ambassadorship to India,
South Africa or Israel. Because it offered "a unique
and extraordinary kind of challenge," as Lewis
recounted in his 1998 oral history for the Association
for Diplomatic Studies and Training, he chose Israel.
That decision proved momentous.

From the time he arrived in Tel Aviv on May 18,
1977, Ambassador Lewis was an active participant
in the Israeli-Egyptian diplomatic breakthrough.

Though he modestly described himself as a mere "postman" relaying messages from the Israeli government to Egyptian President Anwar Sadat prior to Sadat's historic visit to Israel on Nov. 19, 1977, Lewis was intimately involved in the negotiations between the two countries.

President Jimmy Carter (quoted by G.R. Berridge in *Diplomacy: Theory and Practice*) said that he always looked forward to reading Lewis' analyses on Israel, which he found both enlightening and helpful. Few are the American diplomats whose cables reach the desk of the U.S. president. Fewer still are those whose cables he reads with interest.

Carter summoned Lewis to participate in the Camp David Summit, which he convened in September 1978. Those talks would lead to the signing of the Framework Agreements for Peace between Israel and Egypt on Sept. 17, 1978. Lewis had been involved in the secret diplomatic discussions aimed at preparing the U.S. delegation for the crucial conference.

A Good Beginning

Following the Likud Party's electoral victory on May 17, 1977, Amb. Lewis urged the Carter administration to treat the new prime minister, Menachem Begin – widely regarded as obdurate and extremist – gently. Honey was preferable to vinegar, he stressed.

As Begin prepared to make his first official visit

to Washington as prime minister, National Security Adviser Zbigniew Brzezinski urged the president to tell Begin in no uncertain terms that his positions on the future of the West Bank and Gaza were totally unacceptable. Lewis reiterated that adopting a harsh line with Begin would be counterproductive. Fortunately, that view prevailed, and the visit was crowned with success.

There is perhaps no stronger indication of how well Lewis performed his duties in Tel Aviv than the fact that just days after his November 1980 electoral victory, Ronald Reagan asked Lewis to stay on in Israel. That was an almost unprecedented vote of confidence in a career diplomat, particularly one named to his post by a president of another political party.

Amb. Lewis was the first foreign representative to hear from Prime Minister Begin that the Israeli Air Force had destroyed Iraq's nuclear reactor on June 7, 1981. He was also intimately engaged in the diplomacy surrounding Israel's Lebanon War, which began in June 1982.

It was under President Reagan that Lewis was instructed to undertake perhaps the most uncomfortable task of his ambassadorship. In August 1982 he was instructed to convey to Prime Minister Begin, while the latter was on vacation in northern Israel, the contents of what would be known as the Reagan Peace Plan. This proposal had been prepared with the active participation of Saudi Arabia, Egypt and Jordan – but without Israel.

Begin was furious, but Pres. Reagan unveiled the plan anyway on Sept. 1, 1982. As Lewis predicted, it failed to advance the cause of peace. The episode did not lessen Begin's personal affection for Lewis, or his admiration for the envoy's professionalism.

Professional Diplomacy

Beyond the realm of private diplomacy, where Lewis excelled, he was a very popular figure in Israel. Warm, accessible and charming, he frequently dressed casually, in keeping with the informality of Israelis, and attended sports events. And even though the ambassador could barely speak a word of Hebrew, many Israelis thought he was Jewish, which he wasn't.

Lewis had a singular ability to comprehend the most intimate fears harbored by Israelis, to grasp the essence of their yearnings. He was especially adept at dealing with Israeli political leaders. He forged a close relationship with Begin and became a good friend of other politicians, notwithstanding their diverse political leanings and their different personalities.

Samuel Lewis' ambassadorship in Israel demonstrates that a professional diplomat can have an important influence on the shaping of foreign policy. Beyond the input Lewis was able to bring on occasion to the actual formulation of foreign policy, he managed to enhance his country's image, values and interests by the force of his personality and through his singular diplomatic style. For that and much more, both the United States and Israel owe him a debt of gratitude.

Originally published in The Foreign Service Journal, January/February,

2016

JFK Was a Legend in His Own Time

It is said that John F. Kennedy became a legend because of the way he died. Actually, he became a legend because of the way he lived. He turned into a myth due to his tragic death; by then, he had already been a legend for quite a while. As we approach the fiftieth anniversary of Kennedy's greatest triumph – his handling of the Cuban Missile Crisis – it's important to keep that in mind.

Kennedy was the youngest ever person to be elected president of the United States. He was the first Roman Catholic to assume the highest political post in a country steeped in a Protestant ethos. He was a war hero. He was handsome. When he first entered the White House, after being sworn in, he was accompanied by a beautiful, Hollywood-like wife and two little children. When was the last time the people of the United States have witnessed such a scene? JFK represented a generational change, no less than a political one. Not only was he the youngest person ever to be elected president, but his entourage of advisers was striking for its youth.

Kennedy's election ignited a sense of hope reminiscent, in part, to what took place following the election of Barack Obama in 2008. Obama, too, is young and handsome, with two little children and a young wife. Moreover, he's the first African American to be elected president, no less of a feat than having a Roman Catholic elected back in 1960. Both studied at Harvard. Both chose as vice presidential candidates two senior and experienced senators. The similarities, though, stop there. Kennedy came from a very wealthy family; Obama does not. Kennedy came from a socially privileged background; Obama does not. Kennedy was a war hero; Obama is not. However, it should be stressed that being a war hero back then, with World War II still fresh in the minds of most people in the U.S., was an asset; not being a war hero in 2008 or 2012 is certainly not an obstacle.

John Kennedy's father, Joseph, was a pivotal figure in his life. Ambitious and resourceful, Joseph had high hopes for his children. He wanted them to reach the highest echelons of American politics. The elder Kennedy, despite his Irish Catholicism, served as ambassador to Great Britain from 1938 to 1940, displaying a sympathetic attitude towards Nazi Germany. His anti-Semitism was notorious. What's striking is that his children did not follow in his footsteps. Indeed, they were all known for their positive disposition to Jews, going far beyond mere political expediency. Further, John himself was ever cognizant of the perils of appeasement, taking Britain's and France's policy towards Nazi Germany in the 1930s as a warning sign. Joseph had been a supporter of that policy and had expressed his concern that the Jews in the U.S. had pushed FDR to war with Germany.

In shaping foreign policy, particularly during the Cuban Missile Crisis, Kennedy tried to learn from history. Interestingly, and perhaps in contrast to many other people of his generation, he attempted to learn not only from appeasement but also from the European crisis that led to the outbreak of World War I (he was reportedly a great fan of Barbara Tuchman's *The Guns of August*). From the crisis of the '30s, he learned that totalitarian states bent on aggression should be stopped and not appeased. From the events preceding the First World War he learned that if a crisis is not handled with care, events can quickly spiral out of control.

In the realm of foreign policy, Kennedy's youth became an obstacle when domestically it had been an asset. The Soviet leader, Nikita Khrushchev, seemed to have thought that Kennedy was inexperienced and could be easily challenged and beaten. This, along with the disastrous Bay of Pigs invasion, was one of the catalysts which led Khrushchev to decide to install nuclear missiles in Cuba, igniting the worst crisis of the Cold War.

Although widely seen as an American victory, the end of the crisis was never portrayed by Kennedy and his advisers as such. Indeed, the president urged his advisers not to gloat about it; an important lesson for any leader who wishes to prevent the seeds of resentment being sown at the moment of victory. Where a small, monolithic group of advisers held sway in shaping policy before the Bay of Pig invasion, a more diverse and heterogeneous group advised the president during the Cuban Missile Crisis; where dissenting voices were either too timid to express their views or felt intimidated openly to question basic assumptions prior to the Bay of Pigs invasion decision, the president actively encouraged his advisers to convey their opinions and willingly urged them to challenge received wisdom during the Cuban Missile Crisis; where different options and their possible consequences were not examined by Kennedy and his advisers previous to the Bay of Pig invasion decision, six main options and their possible repercussions were studied thoroughly during the Cuban Missile Crisis.

Notwithstanding the quality of the decision-making process, it was no other than McGeorge Bundy, Kennedy's national security advisor, who said in the aftermath of the crisis that luck played an important role in averting war. Perhaps, but luck is blind and thus sometimes needs to be led in the right direction.

The Cuban Missile Crisis gave birth to the concepts of "hawks" and "doves," which are terms used to this day. Those who favored a military strike or urged a more resolute stance were referred to as hawks; those espousing a more restrained policy were known as doves. In fact, though, opinions changed during the crisis as discussions among the president and his advisers evolved. Kennedy himself was in favor of an air strike against the missile bases in Cuba to begin with, only to decide subsequently to institute a maritime blockade around the island, referred to as a "quarantine" to make it sound better and legally more acceptable.

Looking back at his presidency, there can be little doubt that Kennedy's handling of the Cuban Missile Crisis was his major achievement.

His tragic death on November 22, 1963 has produced a variety of "what if?" questions, principal among them: "What would Kennedy have done about Vietnam?"

What is not widely known is that Johnson himself spent many a sleepless night before deciding to send combat troops to Vietnam. He shared his excruciating doubts with Bundy, whom he retained as his national security advisor. A facile image of Johnson resolving to intervene massively in Vietnam in a cavalier, off-the-cuff manner has been on occasion depicted by critics of the war. Historical evidence paints a more complex picture in this respect.

So, what would Kennedy have done? One can't know for sure, of course, but Kennedy was a Democrat hawk, in the tradition of Truman. In contrast to Truman, though, he lived through a crisis with the Soviet Union which came close to deteriorating into a full-scale war. Kennedy learned from the Bay of Pigs what not to do; from the Cuban Missile Crisis he learned what to do. The shadow of nuclear war prompted him – and the Soviets (when Khrushchev was ousted from power in 1964, one of the rationales was his reckless Cuban policy) – to behave with utmost caution.

In Vietnam, however, he might have felt that nuclear war might have been much less of a danger as a consequence of U.S. military action. A Communist takeover of South Vietnam would have been anathema to him. To claim that Kennedy would have been opposed, ipso facto, to military intervention, even if this entailed the demise of South Vietnam as a non-Communist state, is not particularly persuasive.

President Johnson and most of his advisers then thought that military intervention was the most feasible way to try to prevent the defeat of an ally, as it had been in Korea more than a decade previously. The perception prevailing then might have been wrong, but it was earnestly entertained. Why would Kennedy have thought otherwise?

Scholars and laypersons alike will continue to ponder what would have happened if Kennedy had not been killed. The tragedy of his death has clouded somewhat the objectivity of historical inquiry. Many see the myth surrounding the person; a few stress the defects at the expense of the virtues. Indeed, there seems to be a trend to belittle anything Kennedy did as though there were a need to balance the effects of his myth.

Kennedy was an exceptional person, but was he also an exceptional president? His most enduring legacy is to have taught future leaders the importance of having the emotional courage and intellectual honesty to learn from their own mistakes. He did that following the fiasco of the Bay of Pigs invasion. For that, the world owes him a special debt of gratitude.

Originally published in History News Network, August 27, 2012

Did an Historical Analogy Lead Britain to Go to War in the Falklands?

Historical analogy is often used by decision-makers when faced with a new situation. As they shape foreign policy, decision-makers resort to history as a ready-made means to learn from it and/or as a tool to be deployed in diplomacy. Historical analogy helps them understand better a new event, although they might on occasion reach the wrong conclusions from it. That's why they also use it in attempting to elicit support: historical comparisons can be an effective tool in persuading both the domestic and foreign audiences of the rightness of their stance. Thus, historical analogy can be both a cognitive means to cope with a foreign policy crisis and a marketing device to elicit support.

When the Falklands/Malvinas crisis erupted on the 2nd of April 1982, as a result of the Argentinean invasion of the Falklands/Malvinas islands, historical images played an important part in the shaping of Britain's response to it.

Margaret Thatcher, British Prime Minister during the crisis, resorted to historical analogy in order to stress what she would not do. History represented a guide to her in order to avoid doing things her predecessors did.

Thus, she emphasized to Alexander Haig, US Secretary of State who served as mediator between Argentina and Britain, she would refuse to adopt a similar attitude to that of Neville Chamberlain, the architect of the policy of appeasement towards Nazi Germany. A different attitude would be displayed towards the Argentinean dictator in 1982 than towards the German dictator in 1938, she stressed. Thus, in this case, Thatcher both drew a lesson from this historical analogy and made use of it in order to emphasize her stance and persuade her interlocutor.

No less pronounced was the image of the Suez Crisis of 1956 among the key British decision-makers.

The Suez Crisis cast a shadow in the background of the decision-making process. For Thatcher, it constituted a blot in British History that must be remedied and never repeated. For others in the War Cabinet, the Suez Crisis represented a warning sign: if the Task Force is sent to the Falklands Islands, and diplomacy fails, force must be used without hesitation so that the failure of Suez is not repeated in the South Atlantic.

The Suez Crisis was thus paradoxically both a call for caution and for will.

It's interesting to note, in this context, that historical analogy played an important part in the shaping of policy during the Suez Crisis as well.

As it did with Thatcher herself during the Falklands

Crisis, the image of the policy of appeasement of the 1930s loomed largely among the key decision-makers, such as Prime Minister Anthony Eden. Having lived through the events of the 1930s and 1940s, British politicians were prone to draw on the events of those years to highlight the danger represented by then Egyptian President, Gammal Abdel Nasser. Indeed, the Labour opposition was no less explicit in its historical analogies with Nazi Germany than the Conservative Party then in power. Similarly to Thatcher, Eden found the analogy to the 1930s both intellectually instructive and diplomatically useful. He used it, for instance, in his correspondence with then US President Dwight Eisenhower.

Decision-makers tend to make historical comparisons with events that either they or their parents have lived through. Thus, during the Falklands Crisis, the two main events drawing historical analogy from British ministers was the policy of appeasement of the 1930s and the Suez Crisis of 1956.

In a sense, it can be argued that the repercussions of the two analogies were different. Whereas the comparison with the appeasement policy in the 1930s entailed a decision to do things differently, the comparison with the Suez Crisis of 1956 implied not only a decision to do things differently, but also an expectation that a third party, i.e. the United States, should behave differently than it did during the Suez Crisis.

In other words, for the Suez Crisis not to be repeated, the United States, and not only Britain, would need to conduct itself differently than it did then.

In 1956, the United States said it agreed, in principle, with Britain's stance opposing the unilateral nationalization of the Suez Canal Company by Egypt. However, both in private and in public, the US Administration stressed it was equally opposed to the use of force aimed at reversing it. Such a stance did not help enhance the chances of success of the diplomacy then being conducted by the United States aimed at finding a peaceful solution to the crisis. After all, if Nasser knew that the US was opposed to the use of force, why should he concede?

When Britain and France did resort to force, the United States came out vehemently against them, in a manner not seen among those allies either prior or since Suez. Ultimately, this led to the British deciding to quit before they had finished their military undertaking.

The Suez Crisis became a national trauma in the British collective conscience. Suez became a by-word for national humiliation. The British decision-makers in 1982 were determined not to repeat it. Winston Churchill is quoted as having said that he wasn't sure whether, had he been Prime Minister during the Suez Crisis, he would have ordered a military operation as his successor, Antony Eden, did. However, had he done so, Churchill added, he wouldn't have stopped it until it had finished. This was the lesson Thatcher and the War Cabinet learned from the Suez Crisis. If a decision was made to send the Task Force to the Falkland Islands, unless an acceptable diplomatic solution was reached, the military undertaking wouldn't be stopped until it was over.

Britain and France had gone along with every diplomatic proposal advanced by the United States in 1956 so as to avoid a military confrontation. By doing so, they had agreed not to return to the status quo ante that prevailed prior to the unilateral nationalization of the Suez Canal by Nasser. However, by opposing the use of force under any circumstances, the United States left Britain and France essentially two options: to accept the fait accompli by Nasser or to resort to an independent course of action.

During the Falklands Crisis, though US President Ronald Reagan did ask Thatcher to pledge she would foreswear the use of force, he did so privately and was careful not to put obstacles in the way of US mediation between the parties.

When the British Task Force began its military campaign, Reagan asked Thatcher to interrupt it and give diplomacy a further chance. Again, this was done behind the scenes, not in public.

When diplomacy failed, the US came out clearly in favor of Britain. This was in stark contrast to what had happened during the Suez Crisis. Then, following the failure of the diplomatic effort, with which Britain had fully collaborated, the United States never came out publicly in favor of the British stance as it did during the Falklands Crisis.

Certainly, it should be stressed that whereas the British were very open with their US ally during the Falklands Crisis, they were less than candid when deciding to resort to force during the Suez Crisis. Of course, the British could argue that US policy led them to act as they did in 1956. However one might interpret it, the fact remains that the US behaved differently in 1982 than it did in 1956; in a sense, so did Britain.

Originally published in History News Network, May 4, 2014

Did Shimon Peres Make a Difference?

There is a long-running dispute in the philosophy of history as to the role of the individual in shaping history. On one extreme, we have Thomas Carlyle (1795–1881), the Scottish writer and historian, who elevated the individual's role in shaping events to an almost mythical level. He believed that history was shaped to a considerable extent by individual heroes. On the other extreme, we have Georg Wilhelm Friedrich Hegel, the German philosopher (1770–1831), and thinkers such as Karl Marx (1818–1883) and Herbert Spencer (1820–1903), who believed in forces and trends that went much beyond any individual in determining how history unfolded. They ascribed a limited role to the individual in shaping history.

Although the mythical view espoused by Carlyle would hardly fit him, there is no doubt that Shimon Peres is a vivid example that an individual can play an important role in shaping history.

Already by his twenties, Peres was one of the main architects of the special relations between Israel and France in the 1950s. During those years, he secured badly-needed weapons from France and was a central figure in designing and implementing the policy leading to the construction of Israel's nuclear power plant. Peres was one of the main instigators leading to the creation of a military industry in Israel. It would be well-nigh impossible to write about Israel's national security policy in general, and with reference to the 1950s and early 1960s in particular, without mentioning the name of Peres as one of the principal individuals responsible for shaping it.

Peres was the right-hand man of Israel's first Prime Minister and Defence Minister, David Ben-Gurion. As such, he was afforded ample political support to pursue the policies aforementioned. Peres served as Director General of Israel's Defence Ministry and subsequently as Deputy Minister of Defence. He worked closely with Ben-Gurion, whom he deeply admired. Peres was fortunate to have a strong and dominant individual like Ben-Gurion as his boss and Ben-Gurion was lucky enough to have a resourceful and creative individual like Peres on his side. Indeed, this proves that propitious circumstances can certainly help an individual leave his or her mark on history. In this case, an individual who had a significant role in shaping events like Ben-Gurion created the right conditions for another individual like Peres to wield a considerable influence in molding reality.

Peres was for almost fifty years a Member of the Knesset (Israeli Parliament). He served, among other posts, as Minister of Defence, Foreign Minister, Finance Minister and Prime Minister. He was President of Israel from 2007 to 2014.

As Foreign Minister, Peres was the main driving force behind the Oslo Accord of September 1993 which brought about a mutual recognition between Israel and the Palestinian Liberation Organization (PLO) and the withdrawal of Israeli forces from areas inhabited by Palestinian Arabs in the West Bank and Gaza as an interim solution pending final-status negotiations. Indeed, Itzhak Rabin, who served then as Prime Minister, was somewhat skeptical that the secret negotiations taking place in Oslo would lead to an agreement. The Oslo Accord would have been politically impossible without the support of Rabin, but without Peres the negotiations leading to it would not have taken place.

As a consequence of the agreement signed with the PLO, Peres became very optimistic about the regional outlook. He wrote and talked about the emergence of a new Middle East in which peace and reconciliation would replace war and conflict and economic prosperity would spread all over the region. He went so far as to declare that the study of history would become irrelevant as history was the story of wars and conflicts and children in Israel would not be able to relate to it. He said to a group of Israeli children in 1994 that when they reached the age of eighteen they would not serve in the Israel Defence Forces, but rather in the Peace Defence Forces.

Although reality has proved him wrong in this respect, Peres continued to delineate a vision of peace and reconciliation, though gradually bereft of the fanciful notions that he espoused in the wake of the Oslo Accord. Having won alongside Rabin and the PLO leader Yassir Arafat the Nobel Peace Prize, Peres gradually became identified, both in Israel and abroad, with a dovish agenda. He was received all over the world as a messenger of peace. Peres was enormously popular in the chambers of power. He was the Israeli most people in Europe and North America liked to identify with: dovish, with an optimistic vision of peace, espousing an agenda of scientific ingenuity and technological progress. His suave and sophisticated demeanor enhanced the image he carefully cultivated, which so enchanted people all over the world.

Bearing in mind the obvious differences in character and circumstance, not unlike Richard Nixon, Peres, who had been a controversial political figure in Israel for many years, managed to re-brand himself into a coveted world-leader and popular fatherly figure in Israel during the latter part of his life.

The philosopher Sidney Hook (1902–1989), described two kinds of individuals in history: The Eventful individual and the Event-making individual. The first is responsible for changes that could have been effected by another person in his place; the latter is responsible for changes that only he could have effected.

Was Peres an Eventful or Event-making individual?

In a way, it could be argued that he was both. Although a singular person, Peres was hardly the almost mythical figure his admirers make him to be. Paradoxically, his deeds when he was a lesser known political figure in the 1950s and early 1960s make him an Event-making individual. Likewise, his role in the Oslo Accord, make him an Event-making individual. However, to claim that his whole life render him into an Event-making person would be rather simplistic. Peres was a larger-than-life figure, especially when he used to work behind the scenes and under the leadership of someone else who was willing to afford him freedom of action.

Originally published in History News Network, September 29, 2016

Only One Occupied Country in Europe Rose to the Defense of Jews During World War II.

Seventy years ago this year World War II came to an end. Alongside the collective sigh of relief in Allied countries that the most brutal war humanity had ever witnessed was over, there was as well a sense of disbelief at the sight of the concentration camps, the existence of which to be sure had been well-known to the Allies.

Humanity had not witnessed anything resembling the Holocaust. A systematic, rational, industrial plan designed to eliminate completely an entire people from the face of the earth, the Holocaust was to become an exceptional phenomenon in History. Carried out by one of the most cultured nations the world had ever known, the Holocaust would turn out to be a distinctive story of genocide.

Within this unique event, unique individuals emerged who were willing to risk their lives in order to save the life of a Jew. The most well-known of them all was Raoul Wallenberg, the Swedish diplomat, who is credited with having saved, directly and indirectly, the lives of tens of thousands of Jews in Hungary. To be sure, there were many others. Wallenberg in a sense was *primus inter pares*, first among equals. His fate remains a mystery to this day. At the end of the war he was taken by Soviet forces never to be seen again.

Alongside these singular individuals, there was a singular nation that, as a collective endeavor, saved most of its Jews: Denmark.

In a sense, the role played by Denmark was distinctive, different from anything else known to us during the Holocaust.

To begin with, contrary to what happened in other countries, Denmark's populace acted collectively, spontaneously and in an organized manner in order to save its eight thousand Jewish compatriots.

Further, the person to whom the surviving Jews of Denmark owed their lives, apart from the Danish people, was a German official, Georg Ferdinand Duckwitz, who revealed to the Jewish community his government's plan to deport the Danish Jews to concentration camps. This was on the 28th of September 1943. Indeed, faced with disbelief on the part of the Jews, Duckwitz insisted that his information was true and that he was not trying to deceive them.

Also, in an unprecedented manner in those years, Danish fishermen ferried seven thousand and two hundred Jews to Sweden in a coordinated action that saved the lives of most of Denmark's Jews.

Still, almost five hundred Jews were sent to the Theresienstadt Ghetto in Czechoslovakia. However, all of those Jews, but fifty one of them, survived the Holocaust as well due largely to the Danish representations to Germany, enquiring for the well-being of the deported Jews.

The Danish case proved that a collective, spontaneous and organized endeavor aimed at saving Jews could be successful, even in the face of German might and determination.

True, on the whole, the attitude displayed by Nazi Germany toward Denmark was more benevolent than the attitude shown to most other nations in Europe. Indeed, German occupation in Denmark was relatively mild (in Nazi terms).

Nevertheless, when it came to the Jews of Denmark, Germany was no less virulent in its determination to eliminate them, once the decision was taken, than it was in other cases throughout Europe and beyond. This is where the role of Denmark's non-Jewish population becomes so exceptional, and indeed so crucial. Without them, the Danish Jews would have perished as other Jews elsewhere did.

There were many cases of individuals who tried to save Jews during the Holocaust. These were individual examples of heroism. The Danish case is singular in that it was a collective, nation-wide effort.

There have been a few myths attached to the Danish story. For instance it has been said that Denmark's king wore a yellow Star of David badge in public to identify himself with Jews who were compelled to wear such a badge to distinguish them from the non-Jewish population by the German occupying forces. This is apparently untrue. It never happened, so far as we know.

Further, some of the Danish fishermen who actually conveyed Jews to safety in Sweden were apparently paid to do so.

Notwithstanding the myths and partial truths, Denmark's case is still unique in the context of the Holocaust.

In the darkest hour in Jewish history, indeed in human history, the people of Denmark kept a candle of dignity alight, a candle which can be seen in the distance today, seventy years after the end of World War II, as clearly as it was then.

Originally published in History News Network, August 9, 2015 and reproduced by TIME Magazine, August 10, 2015

What's Wrong with Calling ISIS Medieval?

It is in vogue today to refer to the acts of the Islamic State (IS or ISIS, as it used to be known before) as Medieval, or taken from the Middle-Ages.

The Daily Express, for instance, in a headline on the 21st of June 2014, warned its readers of "The New Dark Ages: The Chilling Medieval Society ISIS Extremist Seek to Impose in Iraq."

Recently, the International New York Times carried an article entitled, "With Videos of Killing ISIS Sends Medieval Message by Modern Method," (September 7, 2014)

These are only two examples out of many. Referring to the acts of IS and other Islamic terrorist groups as reminiscent of the Middle-Ages has become quite common in the so-called western media.

The term Medieval denotes a period of time in which society was backward and cruel. The Middle-Ages represents a dark historical landscape far away from the enlightened modern consciousness. Thus, by depicting the terrorist acts carried out by IS as Medieval and the world-view it wishes to impose as belonging to the Middle Ages the media in the democratic world distances IS from the contemporary international setting. IS belongs to a far away period.

Well, it does not. To believe it does is to engage in historical denial.

It is all too facile to attribute the beheading of innocent people in front of TV cameras and a zealous ideology to a distant medieval period.

Acts of brutality and a totalitarian world-view were prevalent to a much greater degree in the 20th century than in the Middle-Ages.

The Middle-Ages knew nothing like Nazi Germany under Adolf Hitler or Communist Russia under Joseph Stalin, even if the huge gaps in technology are taken into consideration. Indeed, the Khmer Rouge in Cambodia carried out acts of unspeakable brutality against its own citizens without having recourse to any advanced technological means to do it. The world-view of Pol Pot, the Khmer Rouge leader, was certainly not more enlightened than that of Abu Bakr al-Bagdhadi, the leader of IS.

Al-Baghdadi's declaration of a Caliphate may be an excuse to justify references to the Middle-Ages in this context. However, a careful reading of the western press, for instance, indicates that the designation has much less to do with the historical connotations of al-Baghdadi's declaration and much more with the image conveyed by the terms Medieval and Middle-Ages. The aim is not to elucidate, but to impress.

To resort to the all-too familiar derogatory terms Middle Ages, Medieval period, Dark Ages in order to describe IS and warn of its nefarious ideology is both historically dubious and intellectually questionable.

There is something enticing about seeing our contemporary world as enlightened compared to a distant period of time in which a primitive, backward, cruel world-view prevailed.

As the 20th century has amply demonstrated, liberal democracies can coexist with totalitarian regimes, enlightened ideas with backward views, order with anarchy and law with cruelty.

The terrorist acts of the 11th of September 2001 were carried out at the very beginning of the 21st century. A hitherto unimaginable scene of fear, destruction and death in the United States occurred as more and more countries in the international system had been embracing democracy.

IS is not the first revolutionary actor in modern history, wishing to destroy the existing international system by force. It is certainly not the first actor espousing a totalitarian ideology, which tolerates no deviation and obliterates all opposition, real or imaginary. It is hardly the first terrorist group to glorify death and take advantage of the sensibilities of fearful audiences and viewers in democratic countries.

There is no need to travel backwards, hundred of years into history to describe IS's brutality or warn us of its sinister world-view. A much shorter journey into history will suffice.

Originally published in History News Network, September 16, 2014

Chapter 2

The Role of History in Shaping Foreign Policy

Learning from History in Shaping Foreign Policy – A Theoretical Framework

There are two distinct ways to learn from history: *The Chronological and the Analogical*. The first entails the study of a historical process leading to a given point in time. Its aim is to understand better the *causes* of the event/s being assessed. The latter entails the attempt to find out similar historical events to the event with which one has to deal at present. Its aim is to overcome the cognitive hurdle of coping with the emergence of a new actor or event, to facilitate the intellectual challenge of having to define the unknown.

Analogy to Elucidate and to Persuade

A distinction ought to be drawn between the use of historical analogy as a tool *to elucidate* and as a means *to persuade*. The first is aimed at enhancing understanding while the latter at marketing policy. Thus, as an illustration of the first, United States President John F. Kennedy tried to learn from the crisis leading to the outbreak of World War I in order to avoid sliding unintentionally into armed conflict during the Cuban Missile Crisis of 1962. As an example of the latter, United States Secretary of State, John Kerry, resorted to the Munich Agreement of 1938, which led to the eventual disintegration of Czechoslovakia and became a synonym to the perils of the policy of appeasement, when he endeavoured to elicit the support of public opinion both in the United States and in Europe to the intended attack by the United States on Syria in 2013.

To be sure, the same analogy could be used both *to elucidate* and *to persuade*.

Effective and Deceptive Analogy

Historical analogy can be *effective* or *deceptive*. If used with caution, dwelling on similarities *and* differences, realizing that the distinctive nature of each event and personality precludes a mathematical-like formula, it can be *effective*. If used like a mirror endeavouring to find a reflection of the present in the past, it can be *deceptive*.

In this context, it is important to stress the difference between *an event* and *a phenomenon*. The Cuban Missile Crisis was *an event*. An International Crisis is *a phenomenon*. Thus, in order to learn any lessons from the crisis that led to the outbreak of World War I, President Kennedy dwelt on how the mishandling of an international crisis caused an unintended catastrophe. That was the main lesson he wished to learn from it. He didn't think that the Cuban Missile Crisis of 1962 was a reflection of the crisis that led to the outbreak of World War I.

A Deterministic and Probabilistic Analysis

The past is not a certain compass to the future, only a possible guide to it. History affords analytical tools that can serve to assess processes, not to anticipate them as one could in the realm of meteorology. A distinction ought to be drawn in this respect between assessing *the likelihood* of an event occurring or a process unfolding and *the certainty* thereof. History teaches us to be modest in foresight.

In the study of history there is a difference between a *deterministic* and a *probabilistic* analytical perspective. The first negates whereas the latter allows for contingency. Thus, stating that World War I *would have* occurred anyway, sooner or later, denotes a *deterministic* analytical perspective; arguing that World War I *might have* occurred, sooner or later, reflects a *probabilistic* analytical perspective.

To learn from history entails an awareness that events were not necessarily meant to occur. The belief in fate or design that go beyond human choice and objective constraints render *a deterministic* analytical perspective easier to accept. *A probabilistic* analytical perspective implies a non-deterministic approach to the study of history.

Chance and Accident – Cause or Trigger?

Chance and accident are an integral part of history. Their role in the shaping of events cannot be dismissed. The question that arises is whether chance and accident constitute *a cause* or *a trigger*. To ascertain that, Counterfactual History can help. Posing a question such as 'might World War I not have broken out had Archduke Franz Ferdinand not been killed by Gavrilo Princip?' is an example of how counterfactual history can help in assessing whether that particular event was *the cause* leading to World War I or *the trigger* instigating it.

The Role of Choice

In this context, it should be emphasized that the question, "Why has policy X been discarded?" may lead to discover explicitly or infer implicitly the constraints facing decision-makers. The preference for policy Y, rather than X, may have had to do as much with the perception of constraints as with the perception of opportunities. In either case, the existence of *choice* is implied. The assumption by the decision-maker that there was a viable alternative denotes free will, for only by free will can an alternative be discarded.

The existence of constraints does not denote the absence of choice. Choice by its very nature implies not only the availability of an alternative but the existence of constraints, for no decision-maker operates in an environment devoid of limits.

Discarded decisions may be no less revealing than adopted decisions. By dwelling on the options that had been contemplated but ultimately left out, a clearer picture of the decision-making process is thus revealed including the assessments of risks and opportunities entailed in each one.

Thus, for example, to revert to the Cuban Missile Crisis, one can learn not only from the reasoning behind the decision by President Kennedy to institute a quarantine of Cuba, but also from the arguments adduced in discarding the other options that had been considered, such as a full-scale invasion, an aerial attack, a diplomatic approach, and not doing anything.

Learning from history entails a reasoned analysis of the decision-making process as whole, and not only of the decision itself that was ultimately adopted.

Originally published in E-International Relations, April 4, 2017

How to Use Effectively Historical Analogies in Foreign Policy

The comparison made by Ukraine's President Volodymyr Zelensky during his speech to the Knesset has produced, quite rightly, considerable indignation in Israel.

Yoav J. Tenemabum

In a speech he delivered to members of the Knesset, Ukraine President Volodymyr Zelensky made an analogy between Nazi Germany's "Final Solution" to the Jewish Question and what he defined as Russian President Vladimir Putin's final solution to Ukraine.

Furthermore, he made an analogy between the help that was supposedly afforded by the Ukraine people to Jews during the Holocaust and the aid Ukraine was expecting from Israel in its war against Russia.

That was not the first time that President Zelensky and Ukraine representatives had made use of historical analogies in order to elicit international support. Indeed, history and historical comparisons have played a central role in Ukraine public diplomacy.

In his speech before the House of Commons in Britain, Zelensky reminded his audience of the bravery of the British people during the Blitz, paraphrasing Winston Churchill's "We shall fight on the beaches" speech. To the members of the United States Congress, he mentioned the Japanese attack on Pearl Harbor on December 7, 1941, and the terrorist attacks in the United States on September 11, 2001. Before the German Bundestag he made a speech alluding to the Berlin Wall in order to convey his message to the German public.

THE USE of historical comparisons in international diplomacy and in domestic politics in foreign-policy-related issues is hardly new. It didn't commence with the Ukraine crisis of 2022, nor will it end with it. Historical analogy has been used in order to persuade.

Thus, for instance, Israeli politicians have made use of historical comparisons between Iran's policy aimed at Israel's destruction and Nazi Germany's in the 1930s and 1940s.

It should be stressed that such a comparison has been drawn by politicians both from the Right (for instance, Benjamin Netanyahu) and from the Left (for example, Shimon Peres). Indeed, when Peres was asked once whether he truly believed that the Iranian regime was identical to Nazi Germany's, he replied that his comparison did not refer to the nature of the regimes concerned, but to the policies adopted by democratic countries toward them.

When Egyptian president Gamal Abdel Nasser, nationalized the Suez Canal on July 27, 1956, sparking an international crisis, Anthony Eden, Britain's prime minister, both in public and in private, made comparisons between Nasser and the dictators of the 1930s, particularly Benito Mussolini, arguing that the Soviet Union, Egypt's ally, was akin to Nazi Germany. The comparison between Nasser and Adolf Hitler was quite common domestically, both in France and in Britain, also among left-wing politicians.

Historical analogy has been used also to inspire. For instance, during the First Gulf War, following Iraq's invasion of Kuwait on August 2, 1990, and the subsequent military operation of the international coalition headed by the United States aimed at liberating Kuwait, Iraq attacked Israel with Scud missiles. Prime minister Yitzhak Shamir tried to inspire the Israeli people by drawing a comparison between what they were enduring and what the British people had to endure during the German Blitz in World War II.

Arab leaders used to compare Israel to the Crusades in order to inspire the Arab people facing defeat: Zionism and Israel would eventually be defeated and would disappear from the Middle East just as the Crusaders were defeated and disappeared in the Middle Ages. It might take a long time, but the Muslims – the Arabs – would ultimately prevail.

The aim of historical analogy, when used in public, is thus to persuade and/or to inspire.

THE HISTORICAL analogies drawn by the Ukraine leadership tend to be adapted to the audience concerned. Thus, the Holocaust is alluded to when speaking to the Israelis, the Blitz when speaking to the British, Pearl Harbor and 9/11 when speaking to the American people, and the Berlin Wall when speaking to the Germans.

The comparison made by Zelensky during his speech to the Knesset has produced, quite rightly, considerable indignation in Israel. However cruel the actions of the Russian army in Ukraine might be considered to be, to compare them to the Holocaust is historically spurious. To advance a distorted historical narrative of the Ukrainian people as a nation of Righteous Gentiles in order to request Israeli military assistance is also historically false.

The problem with Zelensky's public diplomacy vis-à-vis Israel is that by being founded on a transparently distorted historical narrative, it creates a skeptical, if not altogether negative response.

In order to be effective, the use of historical comparisons in public should be the corollary of a reasoned and serious decision-making process. If taken lightly, it will backfire. The Ukraine example is a clear testimony to that.

Originally published in The Jerusalem Post, March 27, 2022

Foreign Policy and Learning from History

Decision-makers are often said to learn nothing from History. Many of them, however, have; or, at least, have tried to. Prior to the Versailles Peace Conference, following World War I, the British Foreign Office produced a document on the Vienna Conference, which followed the Napoleonic Wars in 1815. The document, written by Charles Webster, British historian and diplomat, was aimed at shedding light on the last big international peace conference that had taken place; what worked – and why, and what didn't work – and why. It could be argued that the outcome of Versailles had precious little to do with the international order established at Vienna. Maybe. But at least the British Foreign Office tried to learn from history. It produced a document the sole objective of which was just that. The disappearance of a whole generation of young people during World War I led statesmen in Britain and France to harbor deep-seated fears of another, even more destructive war. Technological progress had led to the development of air forces capable of reaching deep into enemy territory and dropping lethal weapons on civilians and soldiers alike. The aerial bombardments during the Italian attack on Abyssinia (present-day Ethiopia) in 1935–1936 and the German attack on Guernica on 26 April, 1937, during the Spanish Civil War had given a first, bitter taste of the destructiveness of future warfare. Avoiding war became the ultimate rationale of foreign policy. Maybe they were wrong to let their fears dominate their decisions as they faced the peril of Nazi Germany. They were certainly not wrong in depicting an image of utter destruction, hitherto unknown, concerning a future European war. Statesmen in the 1930s were also motivated by the belief that, in part, World War I came about as a result of a series of misunderstandings and a lack of diplomatic dialogue aimed at averting a war. The policy of appeasing Nazi Germany was partly the result of that lesson. Following World War II, decision-makers in democratic countries had learned that a policy of appeasement with regard to dictatorial regimes was both morally untenable and pragmatically unwise. Indeed, appeasement became a byword for undignified surrender. The rhetoric in the United States during the Cold War, the images depicted in shaping policy towards Communism, were imbued with the lessons learned from the failed diplomacy of the democracies in the 1930s. This was, no doubt, partly aimed at eliciting public support. But it was also due to the fact that many of the people involved had lived through World War II and were determined to avoid the mistakes of their predecessors. One can hardly overstate the influence wielded by the memories of how the failure of Versailles, appeasement, and the subsequent War on decision-makers in the West. One of the most fascinating examples is that of Anthony Eden during the Suez Crisis in 1956. A prominent opponent of appeasement in the 1930s, Eden served as British Prime Minister when Egyptian leader Gamal Abdel Nasser took over the Suez Canal company in a unilateral move. Eden identified Nasser with the dictators of the 1930s. If he were not stopped immediately and without hesitation, Nasser, like Hitler and Mussolini, would continue to expand and become a menace to the whole Middle East. Eden was not alone in thinking in those terms. Although one may ascribe Eden's comparison between Nasser and the dictators of the 1930s to political expediency, there can be little doubt that he sincerely believed in it; indeed, that he was motivated by it. The national trauma of Vietnam led the United States to distance itself from a policy of foreign intervention. The trauma of the hostage crisis in Iran, in turn, tilted the balance again towards a policy of intervention. The invasion of the Falkland/Malvinas Islands by Argentina in April 1982 produced among ministers and members of parliament in Britain a comparison between the Argentinean military government and the dictators of the 1930s. The Argentinean dictators had to be stopped like the dictators of the 1930s. Historical analogies were advanced in this case as well for public consumption, but they also became an additional element in the decision-making process of the British government. The same comparisons with the dictators of the 1930s emerged as regards Saddam Hussein especially during the first Gulf War. Arab leaders have equated Zionism and the establishment of the State of Israel to the Crusades: a foreign invasion with only a transitory existence. On the other hand, Menahem Begin, Israel's prime minister between 1977 and 1983, feared Israel becoming another Czechoslovakia (1938): a democracy surrounded by non-democratic regimes being asked to cede territory under the principle of self-determination and thus putting its own future in danger. Decision-makers do learn from history. Those who protest that they don't, usually mean that they don't learn the right lessons, i.e. the lessons they ought to learn. To be sure, history can serve as a powerfully motivating force, as a guide, or even as an excuse. To learn from history entails a realization that history, contrary to what many believe, does not repeat itself. Historical events or phenomena may seem similar. One may learn by drawing on similarities, not by devising mathematical-like formulae. But even then, the possibility of error is as likely as in any other human endeavor. That is surely a historical lesson one ought to learn.

Originally published in International Affairs Forum, February 2009

Munich's Legacy: Historical Analogy as a Tool in Marketing Foreign Policy

U.S. Secretary of State, John Kerry, made a reference, on two separate occasions, to the Munich Agreement of 1938 as he endeavoured to elicit support for President Barak Obama's policy in Syria.

During a conference call with Democratic Party members of the House of Representatives on the 2nd of September, Kerry told them that they faced a "Munich moment" as they weighed whether to back President Obama's call for a limited military strike against Syria.

Speaking in Paris on the 7th of September, during a press conference, Kerry described the situation in Syria as "our Munich moment."

The Munich Agreement, and the policy of appeasement it represented, is one of the most widely used historical analogies by decision-makers and their advisers in shaping foreign policy, and in selling it to the wider public at home and abroad.

The logic of this comparison runs as follows: a dictator with aggressive intentions has to be stopped, as early as possible, the way the dictators of the 1930s were not. The policy of appeasement that was pursued by Britain and France in the 1930s in order to accommodate those dictators, particularly the German leader, Adolf Hitler, was a failure and millions of people paid with their lives for it.

Following World War II, Munich became a by-word for appeasement, which, in turn, became a by-word for surrender. Just by invoking the term "Munich" both the speaker and his audience knew what was meant by it. Few words in political parlance became so laden with historical connotations as this one did.

Historical comparisons can be employed in the decision-making process as a further tool in order to shape foreign policy. It can also be deployed as a political devise aimed at convincing a domestic audience, or as part of a public diplomacy strategy to elicit international support.

Historical analogies help those who shape foreign policy to deal with a complex situation by simplifying it into a familiar cognitive terrain. The same would be true of the audience being exposed to them. However, the aim of the decision-maker in drawing historical comparisons *in public* as Kerry has done in the Syrian case is not primarily to elucidate, but to persuade. Kerry, in drawing historical comparisons, has been trying to market a policy, not to educate his audience.

To be sure, the implication of his words is that anyone who does not support President Obama's policy is an appeaser. What would you rather be, a Chamberlain or a Churchill?

Simple, perhaps even simplistic, but this is not an intellectual exercise intended to find out the truth, but a marketing device designed to elicit support.

This is not to say that a decision-maker who advances a historical analogy in public does not actually believe in it.

However, policy is ultimately decided upon behind closed doors, not in the full glare of the TV cameras or even in a conference call with members of Congress. When historical comparisons are advanced *in public*, the primary aim is to sell a policy, in the same way that other means of persuasion are used to achieve that goal.

Decision-makers can make use of history in shaping foreign policy in two different ways: one by analogy, the other by chronology. In other words, they can either compare a historical case with a present situation by endeavouring to find common features between the two or learn a historical process that has led to the present situation so as to understand it better.

Historical analogy can be effective or deceptive. If used with caution, fully aware of its limitations, drawing the distinctions no less than the similarities entailed in the two cases under discussion, it can certainly help in elucidating a new reality. However, if historical analogy is employed as a mathematical formula, or as a kind of a scientific formula, it might actually distort reality and lead to decisions that are less optimal.

In the same vein, though sometimes effective in eliciting support, historical analogy as a marketing tool tends on occasion to simplify reality more than is warranted and can thus lead to derision by a sceptical audience.

Originally published in OXPOL, The Oxford University Politics Blog,
September 17, 2013

The Case for Historical Advisers in Government

The Sorbonne-educated Israeli historian, Professor Michael Harsegor, has often suggested, in his programme on Galei Tzaal Radio, that every president or prime minister should have a historian serving as personal adviser. He argues that the whole decision-making process would benefit considerably as many mistakes in modern history could have been avoided had a historian been on hand to offer advice. A similar idea was advanced by Professor Sir David Cannadine at the launch of History & Policy in December 2007.

The closest historical example of such a scenario is the appointment of the prominent historian Arthur Schlesinger by US president John F. Kennedy as his Special Assistant at the White House. However, this was an ad hoc appointment; Kennedy did not set up a new unit within the White House headed by a historian. No institutional legacy was left by Kennedy. No permanent post of Historical Adviser to the President was instituted either with the appointment of Schlesinger or in his wake. Indeed, Schlesinger himself resigned in 1964, following Kennedy's assassination. He realised that his role was rendered irrelevant under Kennedy's successor Lyndon Johnson.

Some may suggest Henry Kissinger's name as a further historical example. They would be wrong. Kissinger was appointed by Richard Nixon as his National Security Adviser, not as a historical adviser to the president. The National Security Council had been an integral part of the executive prior to Nixon's election in 1968. Although Kissinger was imbued with a historical, analytical mind, his appointment to the post was due to his expertise in international relations and national security matters.

Neither Nixon, nor any other US president, either before or since, has had a true historical adviser in the White House and no post of historical adviser to the prime minister has been instituted in any major parliamentary democracy. There are historical departments within ministries, such as in the US State Department and the British Foreign Office. Their role, though important, is hardly central in the decision-making process, even of the ministry to which they belong. Would the appointment of a historical adviser have a relative advantage over any other adviser?

Historians know about the future as much as any other person. The past is not a certain compass to the future, only a possible, general guide. History provides analytical tools that can serve to assess processes, not to anticipate them. One of the salutary lessons history can teach is to be modest in foresight. People usually learn from their last similar experience. That may lead to coherent historical parallels, not necessarily to a better judgment about the policy that ought to be adopted.

History is the tale of the singular. Comparisons are valid, indeed sometimes useful and enlightening. On occasion, comparing one event with another, one leader with another, may help to clarify, sharpen and better understand the issue under discussion. However, as a scientific device, historical analysis is as valid to shape policy and anticipate events as other forms of analysis. Historians are no more immune to making political mistakes than anyone else.

Nevertheless, a historical adviser might have a relative advantage, beyond the preparation of background papers on the history of issues under discussion, in shaping the perceptual and implementation stages of policy.

Leaders and their advisers tend to perceive reality, more often than not, through historical lenses. They engage in historical analogies to help them digest new facts by comparing them with already known events. Usually, historical analogies are drawn by leaders and their advisers for political reasons, to elicit support both at home and abroad for a policy adopted.

The historical adviser would have the tools to elevate these historical analogies to the realm of coherent analysis. He or she could introduce a broader range of options, when it comes to historical comparisons, while cautioning against the dangers of facile analogies. The historical adviser could stress that history does not repeat itself. Paradoxically, he or she could advise leaders on the limitations of history as an instrument in the decision-making process.

The problem, of course, is that a leader may start by employing a historical comparison for political reasons and then be gradually convinced of its truth. The difference between historical analogy as a political tool and as a guiding principle in the shaping of policy can easily become blurred. A leader may truly believe in the analogy employed to advance the cause of a policy already adopted. The historical adviser should have a direct input, to give coherent shape to the historical comparison before it is publicly put forward.

In these ways, historical advisers could be a welcome addition to the decision-making process of a head of government. But only if the leader concerned could accept the need for the historian to have a central role, not in deciding policy, but in helping to shape it, from the distinctive perspective that only a historian can bring.

Originally published in History and Policy, October 10, 2009

Chapter 3

Theory and International Relations/Diplomacy

Diplomacy Is the Art of Enhancing Power

Henry Kissinger has written that "Diplomacy is the art of restraining power."

However, History has shown that Diplomacy can be the art of *enhancing* power. Kissinger himself was a protagonist in such a diplomatic exercise when US diplomacy with regard to Communist China in 1971–1972 could be said to have enhanced US power in the international arena.

By engaging both in secret and open diplomacy to effect a rapprochement with Communist China, a country with which the United States had not had diplomatic relations since 1949, the year the Communist took power, the administration of President Richard Nixon was to change, in a sense, the principal feature of the bi-polar international system into a tri-polar one, thus enhancing US diplomatic leverage. Diplomacy in this case *enhanced* US power in the international arena.

Diplomacy can be said to be the art of restraining *force*; force being an element of power, but hardly its sole manifestation. If by power one means *influence* and the ability to project it, then the proposition suggested in the preceding clause seems to be more accurate compared to what Kissinger has argued.

In his article, "The Concept of Power," the late

Robert Dahl, of Yale University, one of the foremost experts in political science, defined power as follows: "A has power over B to the extent that he can get B to do something that B would not otherwise do." Dahl's definition became widely quoted in academia and beyond.

Of course, power as *influence* can be manifested by persuasion rather than coercion. In this context, the definition of Soft Power, a term coined by Harvard University political scientist Joseph Nye, might be more appropriate. He defined Soft Power as "the ability to affect others through the co-optive means of framing the agenda, persuading, and eliciting positive attraction in order to obtain preferred outcomes".

The definition of power as *influence* may have a strong element of *force* in the background, either explicitly or implicitly directed at a specific actor or as a further source of power.

In this respect, it could be argued that diplomacy helps to create propitious circumstances to employ *force* and thus becomes a further element of *power*.

Thus, for instance, when in May 1967, Egyptian President Gamal Abdel Nasser ordered the United Nations peace-keeping forces out of the Sinai Peninsula, closed the Strait of Tiran to Israeli shipping and sharpened his rhetoric against Israel, the Israeli political leadership, against the advice of many of its generals, who urged an immediate military attack, undertook a diplomatic campaign aimed at averting war by requesting the international community to exert pressure on Egypt to revert to the *status quo ante*.

Wishing to prevent war, Israel's prime-minister, Levy Eshkol, realized that if resort to arms became inevitable, diplomacy had to be employed to the fullest possible extent so as to create the propitious international circumstances to avert criticism and elicit support.

In this case, as far as Israel was concerned, diplomacy became a means to restrain *force*, to begin with, and then to enhance *power* by creating the best possible international conditions to resort to *force*.

A similar argument could be advanced with regard to Britain's reaction to the invasion of the Falklands/Malvinas islands by Argentina on the 2nd of April, 1982.

Realizing that the fleet which had been ordered to sail to the South Atlantic in the wake of the Argentinean invasion would take a few weeks to reach its destination, the British Government, headed by Margaret Thatcher, agreed to engage in diplomacy with a two-fold objective: to avert a military confrontation with Argentina and, if this proved impossible, diplomacy was to become a means not only to *restrain* force, but also to *enhance* power by eliciting international support for the use of military force to revert to the *status quo ante*.

Furthermore, diplomacy could also enhance

power by creating military alliances aimed at deploying *force* if necessary.

In this context, it may be worth quoting the definition of Smart Power, a term usually associated with Joseph Nye, by the Center for Strategic and International Studies in the United States: "an approach that underscores the necessity of a strong military, but also invests heavily in alliances, partnerships, and institutions of all levels to expand [...] influence and establish legitimacy [...]."

Thus, when NATO was set up in April 1949, diplomacy was used to enhance *power* by forging an alliance the aim of which was to convey willingness to deploy *force* should the need arise. To be sure, it could be argued that a resort to diplomacy in this case was aimed at restraining *force*, for the ultimate objective was to prevent war by conveying a readiness to engage in it.

It should be further noted that diplomacy could unintentionally lead to a perceived reduction of *power* as it is deployed in order to restrain *force*.

The example that comes to mind is of the appeasement policy adopted by Britain and France towards Nazi Germany in 1937–1938. By actively pursuing a diplomacy aimed at averting war, British and French *power* were paradoxically perceived by Germany to have been reduced. Adolf Hitler himself was quoted as having said a year later, prior to Germany's invasion to Poland, that, based on his personal experience, the British and French leaders were little worms. One could hardly think of a clearer image of *reduced power* than this one.

Thus, to summarize, diplomacy is the art of restraining *force* and enhancing *power*, with the unintentional effect on occasion leading to a *reduction of power*. The distinction between *force* and *power* in this context is as important as the clear understanding of the interconnection between the two in a fluid and changing international context.

Originally published in E-International Relations, February 22, 2022

International Relations: It's Time to Revise How We Talk About Revisionist Powers

Historians and political scientists have traditionally divided countries into status quo and revisionist powers. The former tend to accept the existing international system as it is, while the latter reject the prevailing legitimacy of the international system and seek to alter it considerably or to overthrow it entirely.

I would argue that there is a conceptual problem in ascribing the term revisionist to describe the respective foreign policy goals to international actors, such as Napoleonic France, modern Iran, and Fidel Castro's Cuba. Revisionist, after all, derives from the verb to revise, i.e. to change, to modify, which does not exactly reflect the intentions behind the territorially expansionist and politically hegemonic policies of either power or, indeed, of any other so called revisionist power in modern history. In this respect, the term revolutionary, employed by Henry Kissinger and a few other scholars, seems to be a more accurate description.

The revolutionaries behind the French Revolution of 1789 tried to export its ideas to other parts of Europe, both through the pen and the gun. Napoleon's France expanded much further, destroying the classical balance of power that had existed for most of the 18th century. The multi-polar international system that had characterized the pre-Napoleonic period was replaced by a system dominated by one major power wishing to impose its will on all the other actors within it. The foreign policy goals of Napoleon's France could hardly be described as revisionist. This was a revolutionary power intent on destroying the existing international system.

The same concept applies to sub-systems of the international system. Thus, in a sub-system like the Middle East, the current Iranian regime can be said to have revolutionary foreign policy goals, leading it to seek major changes in the region, including the destruction of Israel as a sovereign state. The Islamic Republic of Iran cannot be described as a revisionist power. That would hardly reflect the dimensions of its regional objectives or the means it is willing to employ in order to bring them about.

Fidel Castro's Cuba was likewise a revolutionary actor in the region, hoping to advance the cause of Marxism in its diverse radical forms both in Central and South America and beyond, as in Angola and Mozambique. Taking into account the scope and magnitude of the change resulting from accomplishing its goals, Castro's government cannot be considered revisionist. His efforts to intervene in Angola and Mozambique in the 1970s to help the Marxist guerrilla, in addition to similar efforts undertaken throughout Latin America, make Castro's Cuba a revolutionary actor in the international system.

Moreover, sovereign states are not the only revolutionary actors. Organizations such as Al Qaeda and its various affiliates are revolutionary in nature because they seek to overthrow the existing international system and its underlying norms. In the context of sub-systems, organizations such as Hezbollah in the Middle East can also be described as revolutionary.

It simply does not make sense to define an organization such as Al Qaeda as revisionist or to claim that Hezbollah merely wishes to revise the prevailing order in the region as it calls for the destruction of Israel and the advancement of Iran's regional ambitions.

What matters in this regard is not necessarily the ability of these organizations to implement all their objectives, but rather their intention and willingness to do so. The same determination applies to sovereign states.

Revolutionary actors are not monolithic, nor are status quo actors necessarily static in shaping the political system. Some of the first may be more revolutionary in intention than others and some of the latter may be more satisfied with the existing international or sub-system than others. For instance, a status quo power like the United States was less satisfied with the prevailing status quo under president George W. Bush than it was under the presidency of his father George H.W. Bush.

Following the terrorist attacks in the United States on September 11, 2001, President Bush and his administration shaped a strategy aimed at changing the status quo, both by toppling the Taliban in Afghanistan and Saddam Hussein's regime in Iraq, and by promoting democracy in the Middle East. The aim was not to destroy the prevailing international order, but to change some aspects of it. Thus, although he started his presidency by enunciating that his Administration would not intervene internationally as the Clinton Administration had done, due to 9/11 he altered his policy and transformed the United States, in a sense, into a revisionist power.

Considering the previous points, the term revisionist does not reflect the true nature of the actors to which the term is usually applied. Conceptually a revisionist state or organization may be a status quo actor wishing to introduce some changes in an otherwise acceptable order.

An international actor wishing to change substantially, let alone completely destroy, the existing international system cannot be said to be revisionist. There is a conceptual problem entailed in referring to such an international actor as revisionist, as its aim is not merely to revise the prevailing international order, but to overthrow it.

This post originally appeared on the blog of the

Georgetown Journal of International Relations. It is reproduced with the permission of the author in OXPOL, The Oxford University Politics Blog, November 6, 2012.

Iran and the Threat of Nuclear Weapons: A Response to Kenneth Waltz

In a recent interview with The Diplomat, Professor Kenneth Waltz discussed the advantages of Iran acquiring nuclear weapons.

An eminent and lucid scholar, Waltz committed the error of trying to fit an incorrect piece of a puzzle into a coherent theory.

His theory whereby nuclear powers have never gone to war against each other has, so far, proven to be right. However, trying to extend this fact in a mechanical manner into a future scenario involving Iran is questionable.

To begin with, the leadership of Iran, as distinct from that of any other of the current nuclear powers, has called for the destruction of its enemy as a sovereign entity. It has made it clear, time and again, that its aim is to see Israel destroyed. Further, it has gone so far as to engage in virulent anti-Semitic rhetoric reminiscent of Nazi ideology. The latest statements made by Iran's president and vice president at a United Nations Conference provide clear testimony to that, along with the fact that it is one of the few countries that denies the Holocaust.

Waltz ascribes to the Iranian leadership the same kind of decision-making logic with regard to Israel as he does to the other nuclear powers concerning their rivals or enemies. He seems to imply that the benefit versus cost equation applies in the same manner in all cases.

He may be right. However, considering the clear aims of Iran's leaders and the ideological motivation behind them, he asks Israel and all other powers interested in stability in the region to risk more than is prudently warranted.

Further, even if one were to believe that Iran's leaders can be deterred, a nuclear Iran would be, contrary to what Waltz argues, a more self-assured revolutionary power in the region.

It will feel less, rather than more, constrained to incite its allies against Israel and any other country in the region. After all, even according to Waltz's own theory, Israel would never use its nuclear weapons against Iran even if Hezbollah or any of Iran's other allies repeatedly attacked it. Why should a nuclear Iran be less willing to engage even more vigorously in supporting proxy attacks than it does at present? Iran's immunity would be enhanced as the costs of attacking it are perceived to increase.

Waltz seems to be incredulous that Israel should continue to be the only nuclear state in the Middle East. How can one fathom such a scenario? A nuclear Iran appears to him to be a solution to a problem that does not exist. After all, even if Israel does possess nuclear weapons, the fact remains that it is the only country on the planet that has been threatened with its very existence. Nuclear weapons are an insurance policy against destruction.

For Israel, possessing nuclear weapons is not aimed simply at deterring an attack, but rather at avoiding its destruction. A nuclear Iran would only make this truth even more evident.

This post first appeared on the website of the Georgetown Journal of International Affairs. *It is reposted in OXPOL, The Oxford University Politics Blog, with the permission of the author, August 23, 2012*

International Conflicts: What is the Difference between Risk and Uncertainty?

To answer this question, I'll begin with a few basic statements. Risk is tangible; uncertainty is not. One can define risk, but one can barely delineate the outer layers of uncertainty. Risk can be rendered concrete; uncertainty cannot.

We can identify risk like we do a distant train coming towards us or to a dog barking at us nearby. Of course, the train may change its course before it reaches us; it may slow down or stop altogether. The dog, for its part, may bark without doing anything beyond that. Risk, after all, is not the train which has killed us or the dog that has attacked us. Neither constitutes risk. Rather, the danger perceived to be looming – whether close by or far away – represents risk. The realized danger, so to speak, is no longer a risk.

Uncertainty on the other hand has too many unknown variables. To turn to the examples aforementioned, uncertainty would be akin to us not knowing if the train has already left the station; and if it has, whether it would be using tracks leading our way. Uncertainty would be like knowing there is a dog somewhere in the neighborhood without us having a clue as to whether it would be heading towards us. It might not bark at us at all.

In the same vein, and following a similar logic, one should be careful to distinguish between risk and uncertainty when it comes to international conflicts. To go back in history, the French Revolution of 1789 represented an uncertain event to the other European powers; its outward expansion constituted a risk for them. The rise of the Nazi Party in Germany in 1933 was perceived by the democracies as more of an uncertain event than a risky development. The German conquest of Czechoslovakia in March 1939, however, convinced almost all decision-makers in democratic countries that Germany constituted a risk to the international system.

Of course the difference between a risk and uncertainty may be a matter of perception.

Subsequent to Napoleon's defeat, a conceptual difference of opinion divided the British from the continental powers. Whereas the latter viewed any political revolution anywhere as a risk, the British thought the risk was only in the outward expansion of such a revolution. Thus the British saw uncertainty where the continental powers saw risk.

At the time the Nazis assumed power, Britain's ambassador to Germany, Sir Horace Rumbold, warned his government about the Nazi Party and the threat it presented. He even alerted the Foreign Office in London prior to 1933 of the danger that a Nazi-led government would represent to Germany and European stability. Here, he perceived risk where many others saw uncertainty.

Why is this relevant now? Let's look at Iran. For years, Iran's nuclear programme has been regarded by most democratic countries as uncertain and seen by Israel, and later the United States, as a risk.

Today, most democratic countries tend to agree conceptually that Iran's nuclear programme constitutes a risk, although there is a difference of opinion with regard to the time left and the means to be employed to counter it.

To be sure, uncertainty may be regarded as potentially affording opportunities, such as the so-called Arab Spring was/is perceived by many decision-makers and opinion shapers in the democratic countries.

All of this is a matter of perspective. The distinction between risk and uncertainty can be defined objectively, but, when it comes to the shaping of foreign policy, it is often a matter of perception about whether an event or a process is seen as risky or uncertain. Uncertainty and risk provide different thresholds.

Originally published in OXPOL, The Oxford University Politics Blog,
October 3, 2012

Conceptual Framework: Democratic Peace Theory from The Perspective of The English School Theory of International Relations

One of the most persuasive international relations theories is Democratic Peace Theory (DPT). Both theoretically coherent and empirically solid, DPT has its roots in Emmanuel Kant's famous essay on Perpetual Peace. The main argument, of course, stipulates that liberal democracies do not engage in wars against each other. This has, so far, been empirically proven to be true. The emphasis here is on two key words: stable and liberal. Only states that hold free and fair elections on a regular basis, safeguard the rights of the minority and possess an independent judiciary fall within the province of this definition.

DPT also stipulates that interstate conflicts between two liberal democracies may emerge, but these are settled by peaceful rather than violent means. Moreover, this is not to say that liberal-democracies may not engage in violent conflicts, but that these always involve a non-liberal democratic international actor.

With this understood, my question here is whether DPT can be analysed from the perspective of the "English School" of International Relations. I argue that there is a strong conceptual basis from which to do so.

The English School Theory (EST) is said to be a *via media*, a middle-way, between the Realist Theory and the Liberal Theory. Similarly to the Realist Theory, EST believes that the international system is anarchic. However, it argues that beyond the mechanic-like interactions prevailing within the international system, there is an international 'society' that binds its members through shared norms, interests and institutions. Thus, institutions such as diplomacy, international law and the balance of power, as well as shared norms and expectations, forge a sense of society at the international level.

Professor Barry Buzan at the London School of Economics, one of the most prominent members of the English School, has contended that the international society is divided into two: on the one hand there is a homogenous group of international actors that share a common historical and cultural background, and on the other a group that is linked by a contractual bond. He argues that there are several circles composing the international society: the closer one gets to the core, the nearest one gets to the smallest circle of shared norms, values and interests.

Following the main tenets of EST, as expressed by its classical members, C.A.W. Manning, Hedley Bull, Martin Wight, and as developed further by Barry

Buzan, Richard Little and others, I believe that DST can certainly be analysed through the paradigm of EPT.

What this would suggest is that liberal democracies do not fight each other because they are part of the inner circle of an international society. They share common values, norms, expectations and culture (political culture) that binds them together. In a sense, they are part of a family.

To be sure, the members of this inner circle are not all part of a homogenous social cultural milieu. They share, though, a common political culture that is stronger in its effects on the mutual interactions between them. Thus, the shared political culture has a more permanent impact on the shaping of foreign policy than the differences in social culture.

They form a cohesive group whose common values, shared expectations, and accepted norms are stronger in their effect than the common social cultural values of the major European powers during the period of the Classical Balance of Power in the 18th century. Back then, the socio-political elites had more in common with each other than with members of the lower social ranks in their own respective countries, but not enough to eschew violence and war. Divergent interests and different goals could drive them to violence.

That is not the case with liberal democracies. Interstate conflicts between liberal democracies occur but never assume a violent manifestation, and certainly never descend into a full-scale war. The common values, norms and expectations are a constraint of such magnitude that war is considered to be unthinkable notwithstanding the divergent interests or different goals entailed.

Liberal-democracies are, in a sense, the highest form of a cohesive international society (or inner circle thereof) that has ever emerged in history.

Under this reading, I suggest, EST has an intellectually persuasive and academically coherent analysis of this singular phenomenon.

Originally published in OXPOL, The Oxford University Politics Blog,
December 12, 2012

The Role of the Diplomat in the Modern Era

I t is in vogue to say that in the 21st century, diplomats are a relic of a distant past that is no longer relevant to the way that international relations are conducted today. After all, heads of government and other top officials can deliver messages without recourse to diplomatic messengers. And decision-makers can rely on summit meetings, direct telephone conversations and video conferences, and other communication technologies.

Those espousing this view contend that a short flight or an e-mail message constitutes the bridge linking states – a function once performed by diplomats accredited to foreign governments or working in their own foreign ministries.

Even those who defend the relevance of traditional diplomacy concede that its practice has to be modified. For instance, what was once a politically centered profession has steadily become more oriented to commerce and economics, as globalization and growing economic interdependence require deeper knowledge of such issues, both on the bilateral and multilateral levels.

Still, no matter how well advanced the means of communication, or how often heads of government and foreign ministers talk to each other, the input of individual diplomats at a conceptual, intellectual level cannot be replaced.

Spending years in a certain country, or following developments there, confers invaluable knowledge of the intricacies of its political system, the various dimensions of its domestic base prompting the decisions of its leaders, and the richness of its social structures. No single decision-maker can devote the time and energy required for such a task.

The Value of the Long View

Take, for example, the case of the late George Kennan and his "Long Telegram" of February 1946. Drawing on his many years spent representing the United States government in Moscow, George Kennan cogently explained the nature of the communist system in the Soviet Union and assessed how it would evolve as it expanded beyond its frontiers. On that basis, he urged a policy of containment, which became the basis of U.S. policy towards the Soviet Union for decades to come.

Admittedly, the timing of the document – generated less than a year after the end of World War II removed the principal basis for cooperation between Washington and Moscow – made the Truman administration receptive to its recommendations. However, the sheer intellectual force of Kennan's analysis was rooted in years of hard-won insights into Soviet society and thorough study, conducted by a diplomat with a creatively analytical mind.

Further, a diplomat can enhance the image of his country in the state to which he or she is accredited and avert a crisis by his or her force of personality and engaging diplomacy. Think of U.S. Ambassador to Mexico Josephus Daniels, who was appointed by President Franklin Delano Roosevelt in 1933 at a particularly sensitive moment in bilateral relations.

Ambassador Daniels managed to dispel the ill feeling prevailing in Mexico toward his country. Perhaps his greatest test was the nationalization of the foreign-owned oil industry by the Mexican government in 1938. The prospect of a major diplomatic crisis between the two countries loomed in the horizon. Ambassador Daniels was opposed to any drastic response by the US government, advising it to refrain from undertaking steps that would lead to the collapse of the bilateral relations. Indeed, he stated that, in the long run, a proud national Mexican nation, improving its economic lot, would benefit the US. The Mexican move, he argued, was not motivated by any radical social ideology, but by patriotic, nationalistic ideals. He played an active role in maintaining the fragile relationship stable, going so far as to interfere in the content and timing of official US demarches that would have brought the bilateral relationship to breaking point. The Under-Secretary for Foreign Affairs in the Mexican Government is said to have acknowledged Ambassador's Daniels vital role in this instance by declaring that had it not been for his intervention, Mexico would have cut off diplomatic relations with the US.

He was particularly adept at explaining the position of each country to the other while avoiding, as far as possible, any undue conflict that might arise due the historically emotional background in US-Mexican relations. Certainly, his friendship with FDR enhanced his diplomatic clout with his Mexican counterparts. But had it not been for his diplomatic abilities and his sensitivities toward the delicate thread of Mexican-U.S. relations, however, these might have evolved differently.

An ambassador's style may add an important layer of confidence to the bilateral relations with another country in times of unpredictable change. Samuel Lewis became U.S. ambassador to Israel in 1977 just as the Likud Party under Menachem Begin came to power, following 29 years of Labor Party rule. Ambassador Lewis's engaging personality, his understanding of the Israeli political system, and his unique sensitivity towards the Israeli public, transformed him from a highly respected person into a singularly admired figure, with all its positive repercussions as regards the bilateral relations between the two countries at a sensitive time.

Only Connect

A diplomat can develop a personal relationship with various persons of influence in the country to which he or she is accredited, a relationship that can be nurtured gradually and productively to the benefit of his or her country. A skillful diplomat uses modern technology as a tool to become a patient forger of valuable relationships, a meticulous observer of political and social phenomena, a shaper of images through the force of personality, and a definer of conceptual diplomatic frameworks.

This dimension of a diplomat's work also applies to those working in a foreign ministry. The cumulative wisdom of the professional who handles a specific geographical area or functional issue on a daily basis for years represents a unique contribution to the decision-making process.

Another example comes from diplomats involved in policy planning. The new technological developments in communications have hardly affected the significance of this particular aspect of the diplomatic work. If such a work is, from time to time, belittled by policy makers this has precious little to do with the way new technology has evolved.

By all means, the role of the diplomat has to be considered anew. However, this has to be done not with a view of annulling the irreplaceable task of the diplomat abroad and at home, or confining it principally to commercial activity, but with the aim of enhancing it intellectually and politically.

Originally published in The Foreign Service Journal, January 2010

On the Role of the Modern Diplomat

The work of the modern diplomat entails a singular paradox. A diplomat may feel his or her contribution to the formulation of foreign policy may be limited, and yet his or her role in helping to shape it has actually become more pronounced.

A distinction is hereby made between formulating and shaping foreign policy. The first refers to the decision-making process leading directly to the adoption of a certain policy; the latter applies more widely, to the input aiding in the decision-making process and to the output helping in presenting and arguing on behalf of the policy decided upon. The process of shaping a foreign policy includes that of formulating it; but not vice versa. The formulation of foreign policy is a more focused exercise entailing the manner by which a decision is actually reached (or discarded). The shaping of foreign policy applies in a broader context to include the many dimensions of the decision-making process as well as the manner by which it is conveyed.

The role of the modern diplomat has become more varied and dynamic: conveying to the decision-makers the information and analysis that may assist in determining the strategy to be pursued, on the one hand, and contributing in articulating and molding the manner by which this strategy is to be explained and implemented as a coherent policy, on the other hand.

Modern communication and high technology have rendered the role of the diplomat less central in the formulation of foreign policy and yet have turned it into a more multi-dimensional one in shaping it.

The large number of media outlets, the speed by which information flows, compels the modern diplomat to be apprised of events and to react to them within a time-limit hitherto unknown to diplomats in the past.

The increasing role of public opinion, whether directly or indirectly, in shaping foreign policy require of the modern diplomat to have the ability to anticipate trends, if at all possible, and to try to help shape them in the interests of his or her country, once they have become apparent.

The modern diplomat is increasingly exposed to, and has to deal in a subtle manner with, a variety of professional, social and cultural groups within his or her host country deemed to be important in furthering bi-lateral relations or a broader foreign policy agenda of his or her own country.

Apart from all the aforementioned, the modern diplomat has still to pursue the more classical tasks of dealing with the officials and politicians in the country in which he or she serves. This is one important aspect of diplomacy that has not changed much with the times.

Thus, the modern diplomat has to play a diversified role in a multi-layered environment. It is argued here that his or her tasks in helping to shape foreign policy could be conceptually divided into the following five categories:

Court-Room Diplomacy This entails the work of the diplomat as an advocate for his or her country, arguing in its defense, particularly in times of conflict, whether involving the two states concerned or the diplomat's country with a third party.

Tour-Guide Diplomacy In this scenario, the diplomat is involved in marketing his or her country beyond any political dispute that may prevail either with the country in which he or she serves or with a third party. It is a process which attempts to draw attention to the particularly attractive features of his or her country that may appeal to the varied audience in the host country. This process is aimed at enhancing the image of his or her country with all the accruing benefits entailed in it.

Trader Diplomacy This aspect of the modern diplomat's work involves negotiating with the host country on a range of issues, from the political to the commercial. To be sure, increasingly bilateral and multilateral negotiations tend to be conducted at the level of higher-ranking officials or ministers. The role of the diplomat in this regard, however, is still important.

Five o'clock Tea Diplomacy Entailing the one-to-one dialogue maintained with government officials or representatives of the private sector, it is aimed at conveying messages, exchanging views, clarifying positions, and exploring mutually advantageous opportunities. Usually, these kinds of meetings are held discreetly, even if they are not necessarily meant to be secret.

Didactic Diplomacy A term chosen to depict the role of the modern diplomat as a person who relays information, conveys analyses, and tries to enlighten officials and ministers at home about the pertinent events in the country in which he or she serves. It may refer, as well, to a wider conceptual dimension of the work undertaken by the modern diplomat: a personal credo of the diplomat concerned about general trends, more deep-seated processes, future developments, which may form part of the intellectual basis for the shaping of his or her country's foreign policy.

Some of the five conceptual categories thus mentioned apply to the work of the modern diplomat in different settings. Thus, for instance, Court-Room Diplomacy or Tour-Guide Diplomacy may apply to a one-to-one dialogue with an official, to a lecture at an academic institution or to an interview with the electronic or printed media.

These five categories are advanced with a view to

clarifying the role of the modern diplomat. Rather than refer to the work of the modern diplomat in general terms, a conceptual division as suggested in this article may contribute to further advance our understanding of this important area of both theoretical and empirical study.

There is a misperception regarding the role of the modern diplomat. Some observers confuse the role of the modern diplomat in formulating and in shaping foreign policy. The more limited role as regards the first does not denote any adverse change concerning the latter. Indeed, in a sense, the role of the modern diplomat in helping to shape foreign policy has increased as his or her role in formulating it has decreased. It has certainly become thematically more multi-dimensional and operationally more dynamic.

The five categories proposed in this article, as well as the distinction drawn between formulating and shaping foreign policy, are aimed at delineating a conceptual framework within which, it is hoped, further studies on the role of the modern diplomat may be conducted.

Originally published in American Diplomacy, May 2010

The Success & Failure of Non-Violence

Yoav Tenembaum asks when a policy of
non-violence is feasible.

Non-violence as a policy is based on the moral
postulate that the use of force is inherently
abhorrent, and further, seeks to link non-violence to
concrete political objectives. The question raised in
this article refers, first and foremost, to the viability
of a policy of non-violence, rather than to its absolute
moral merits; but to be sure, the three most prominent
examples of advocacy of a policy of non-violence in
modern history were moved by moral convictions.
The three are Martin Luther King, Jr., Mahatma
Gandhi, and the pacifist movements of the twentieth
century. Martin Luther King's policy represents the
best-known example of a non-violent policy in a
situation where a segment of the population within a
sovereign state is deeply opposed to that state's official
policy or to internally-upheld social conditions. He
and his followers believed that the blatant injustice
against the black population in the Southern states of
the United States of America needed to be challenged
by a series of non-violent steps. By contrast,
Mahatma Gandhi's advocacy of non-violence applied

in a scenario of colonialism, that is, in the context of foreign occupation. Gandhi and his followers sought to oppose British rule in India. By further contrast, the pacifist movements of the twentieth century took place in the contest of inter-state relations. They were against the use of violence in inter-state relations, arguing that war is a morally untenable option in international relations.

Martin Luther King, Jr. and Mahatma Gandhi succeeded, where the pacifist movements did not. The question is, why?

First, King, Gandhi and their followers had clearly-defined and limited objectives. The pacifists, on the other hand, challenged a much wider, more powerful set of interests and tried to attain an Olympian objective of absolute, global peace.

One crucial factor in the success of King and Gandhi's campaigns was the nature of the political systems of the United States and Britain: both were democracies. A non-violent policy has a better chance of succeeding when operating against democratic rather than dictatorial states. Indeed, the chances of either of those two attaining the same results if they had been faced by a regime such as Nazi Germany or Stalin's Soviet Union would have been considerably lower, to say the least. There were non-violent opponents of the Soviet regime in the post-Stalinist era who managed to survive the system; but they did not overcome it. Certainly, the dissidents who adopted non-violent means in their struggle against the Communist regime were indirectly instrumental in effecting changes there, by mobilizing world public opinion and being the focus of attention for human rights groups outside of the country. These effects, though, were not structural in nature, but rather tactical: they did not change the structure of Soviet society itself. Indeed, the most formidable contribution made by these dissidents was in enlightening public opinion outside of the Soviet Union about the true conditions prevailing in it. Evidently then, non-violent struggle may work towards enhancing the awareness of world opinion, particularly in democratic countries, and thus help the cause concerned. A clear contemporary example of this is the campaign by the Dalai Lama concerning Tibet. His non-violent campaigning has had scant effect in China itself – its main impact has been abroad. In galvanising international public opinion, the Dalai Lama has become a symbol for Tibetan liberation, and thanks to this his cause remains alive.

Non-violent protests were ostensibly successful in producing regime change in Eastern Europe after the fall of the Berlin Wall. However, one should be careful not to confuse the manifestations of a change already taking effect, and the causes of such a change, or the forces which allow such a change to take place. That is to say, the Communist regimes in Eastern Europe collapsed because of Michael Gorbachev's decision not to maintain them by force. Once the menace of Soviet intervention disappeared from the political balance sheet in Eastern Europe, the local Communist regimes had no chance of surviving. Thus, non-violence did succeed here, but it was most significantly *Soviet* non-violence, which created the conditions allowing Communism to fall peacefully in Eastern Europe. To be sure, the Soviet Union did not welcome the collapse of Communism in Eastern Europe; it simply did not act to prevent it. Thus, one principle is, non-violent campaigns have a chance of succeeding if faced by a weak opponent which relies for its continued hold on power upon an external factor no longer willing to sustain it.

The power of the non-violent campaign undertaken by Martin Luther King, Jr. was strengthened by his positive message which lacked any shred of vengeance. The philosophy of non-violence espoused by Mahatma Gandhi itself found resonance among the British public, who were averse to political repression by violent means. The British had always been proud of the fact that political reforms in the modern era in Britain were brought about mostly by gradual, non-violent means – in contrast to Continental Europe, in which political changes were produced on various occasions by violent revolutions or civil wars. And to be sure, Britain was overstretched following World War II, with hardly sufficient resources to prop up its vast empire and meet its large international commitments. Withdrawing from India was as much a decision based on British economic and political calculations as the result of Mahatma Gandhi's non-violent struggle.

Non-violence is futile if faced by a force determined to kill the person adopting it. Thus, an active policy of non-violence by Jews during the Holocaust would have been pointless. A Jewish Mahatma Gandhi or Martin Luther King would have ended up in the gas chambers, as many non-violent Jews did. Similarly, non-violence in inter-state relations is futile if confronted by a power intent on destroying the other side. A policy of non-violence in inter-state relations is viable only if there are enough people on both sides to create sufficient pressure to prevent the eruption of violence from either side. Non-violence as a feasible policy, endowed with a strong moral base, has to relate its assumptions to the results it may achieve.

Originally published in Philosophy Now, July/August 2011

The Challenge of Israeli Diplomacy

Israeli diplomacy faces a challenge: on the one hand, it has to project an image of Israel as a powerful country; on the other, it has to project an image of Israel as a vulnerable country. Striking the right balance between the two is perhaps the most difficult challenge facing Israeli diplomacy.

Israel has to convey an image of power to deter and an image of vulnerability to convince. Israel is both powerful and vulnerable; conveying such an image to an international audience, often impressed by images devoid of context, is a particularly daunting task.

Israel is powerful not only militarily, but also technologically, scientifically and economically. Further, it is widely believed that Israel possesses nuclear capacity, though it has never confirmed it. Israel is also vulnerable.

Surrounded by enemies calling for its destruction, Israel is a tiny state with no defensible borders, certainly not in its pre-Six Day War version, having thus almost no margin of error. Israel's first prime minister's dictum that the Arabs can afford to lose as many wars as they want while Israel can't afford to lose even one reflects this geopolitical reality. David

Ben-Gurion's statement explains Israel's tendency to adopt a proactive national security policy. To paraphrase Henry Kissinger, Israel's crucial battle is the first, not the last one.

This should lead Israel to adopt, again to paraphrase Kissinger, a precautionary policy, to take the initiative rather than wait to be attacked.

However, doing that has created serious diplomatic and public relations problems for Israel. To demonstrate that it is vulnerable, Israel has to wait to be attacked. This is the dilemma of a country in Israel's geopolitical situation: having almost no margin of error, diplomatically Israel must wait even though militarily it must not; and even when it does wait, and then reacts, it runs the risk of being leveled as aggressive, engaged in "disproportionate" retaliatory acts.

Thus, Israeli diplomacy must explain Israel's vulnerability in the aftermath of retaliatory acts which supposedly portray a far from vulnerable country.

Israel enjoyed widespread international support when it was perceived to be vulnerable. Thus, prior to the Six Day War, tiny Israel was seen as a vulnerable country fighting the entire Arab world bent on its destruction.

Even under a right-wing government, headed by the seemingly hawkish Yitzhak Shamir, Israel enjoyed considerable international backing during the First Gulf War in 1991 as it was attacked with Scud missiles by Iraq. Of course, Israel did not retaliate, which helped in this regard. Also, Israel was seen to be part of the anti-Iraqi coalition, even if it was not officially so, thus it was easier to identify with Israel's plight.

The last two wars against Hamas and the other armed groups in Gaza highlighted the challenge facing Israeli diplomacy. Due to its vulnerability, Israel has created the anti-missile Iron Dome system, which, coupled with one of the best civil defense organizations in the world, was able to save many lives and spare much destruction.

Thus, while images of destruction were shown from the Gaza Strip Israel could only engage in "what if" scenarios. What would have happened had Israel not had the Iron Dome system? How many dead and wounded citizens would there have been? How much destruction to Israel's infrastructure would have been inflicted as a result of the missiles directed at Israel's civilian centers? Conveying Israel's vulnerability becomes an intellectual exercise which requires an imaginative leap totally unnecessary in the case of clear images of destruction devoid of context, bereft of explanation (which is not to say that those images do not reflect true suffering by the local population on the other side).

Israel is a powerful country precisely because it is vulnerable. If Israel were not vulnerable it wouldn't need to be powerful. Israel's vulnerability becomes more difficult to explain also because the immediate security challenge it faces is from non-state actors perceived to be weaker than Israel. The image of the weak seeking freedom, however distorted it might on occasion be, can easily neutralize the effect of a coherent explanation by the perceived stronger side. To engage in a logical discourse on one's own vulnerability is less effective than portraying a simple image of vulnerability. After all, who is more vulnerable, the one holding a knife or carrying a bomb or even launching a short-range missile or the one wielding the most sophisticated weapons known to humanity? To be sure, if Israel were facing only this security challenge, Israel's strategic position would be considerably better than it actually is. However, Israel has to confront other enemies, and potential enemies, seeking its destruction, such as Iran, Hezbollah, groups affiliated with al-Qaida, Islamic State and others.

Israel's former prime minster Golda Meir once said, "I would rather be alive and unpopular than dead and popular."

The challenge facing Israeli diplomacy is less stark than that, but it is nevertheless difficult to overcome.

Originally published in The Jerusalem Post, January 1, 2015

International Society and Uncertainty in International Relations

The ongoing conflicts between the United States and its allies and Russia and between the United States and its allies and China reflect both the anarchical nature of the international system and the uncertainty with which decision-makers and diplomats have to deal with in attempting to solve the conflicts peacefully.

Uncertainty is not only a feature of an anarchical international system, but also a characteristic of diplomacy involving actors with different cultures and ideologies. The aforementioned conflicts exemplify this. Notwithstanding the intrinsic cases of the parties to those conflicts, the ideological and cultural gaps tend to enhance the uncertainty entailed in them.

Beyond anarchy, the main obstacle to international stability is uncertainty. Indeed, in a way it could be said that what defines international relations is not just the anarchical nature of the international system, but the uncertainty dominating it.

The primary aim of international actors is not to deal with the anarchy at the international system level, but to cope with the prevailing uncertainty in international relations. The first is, after all, an abstract systemic feature whereas the latter is an immediate policy challenge.

The existence of an international society, with shared norms and interests, helps reduce the degree of uncertainty prevailing in the international system. The greater the congruence of norms and interests among international actors the lower the degree of uncertainty prevailing in the international system. Indeed, the more normatively cohesive such an international society is the less adverse are the repercussions of uncertainty in it.

The benefits of a balance-of-power system such as the ones that prevailed prior to the French Revolution and subsequent to its demise is the reduced level of uncertainty in international relations deriving from agreed upon rules and common expectations. It is not just the written agreement or covenant that lowers the level of uncertainty in international relations, but the implicit understanding regarding the acceptable mode of conduct by members of an international society.

This is the advantage in this regard of the Democratic Peace Theory, which suggests that stable parliamentary democracies do not engage in war with each other. Stable parliamentary democracies, sharing the same political culture, are able to lower the level of uncertainty in their relationship, ensuring a more stable bilateral and multilateral interaction on that account. In this case, reduced uncertainty is not circumstantial, but an inherent feature of those relationships.

The *cause* of the Democratic Peace Theory is related to the nature of the internal political system and the prevailing political culture; the *result* is a reduced level of uncertainty leading to an increased degree of stability.

The Democratic Peace Theory in this context can be regarded as a form of a cohesive international society of shared norms and interests founded upon a common political culture.

In a sense, what the balance-of-power system prevailing prior to the French Revolution and following Napoleon's downfall and the Democratic Peace Theory have in common is the *shared assumptions* among the international actors concerned.

Shared assumptions as to the meaning of messages exchanged between two parties *ipso facto* reduces the level of uncertainty; a common political culture considerably enhances the chances of understanding and the consequent probability of reduced uncertainty.

Disparity as to the meaning of messages increases the level of uncertainty in a bilateral relationship. As the gap between the *intention* of A and the *interpretation* of B widens so does the level of uncertainty in their relationship. In other words, what matters in particular in this regard is not the message itself but the *intention* of the party delivering the message and the *interpretation* of the party receiving it; the wider the gap between the two, the higher the level of uncertainty. Thus, beyond common interests and norms, a shared world-view or cultural background may reduce the chances of misunderstanding and thus subsequently of uncertainty.

An international society with shared norms and interests has the advantage of reducing the level of uncertainty in the international system. The actors within it shape decisions based on common assumptions.

It is the nature of such an international society that uncertainty is reduced, though conflicts still prevail. Shared interests and norms help reduce the level of uncertainty by setting a framework within which differences and even conflicts take place.

An international society is not characterized by the lack of conflicts, but by the mode in which those conflicts are handled, the manner by which they are settled.

The effects of a cohesive international society are cyclical: The less uncertain the conditions in the international system are, the less nebulous reality becomes for the decision-maker. The less nebulous reality becomes for the decision-maker, the less uncertain the conditions in the international system are.

These conclusions suggest that facing current conflicts, such as those besetting the United States and Russia and the United States and China, calls for reducing uncertainty. The difficulty entailed in that might be the lack of a common, cohesive normative framework. However, this should not necessarily preclude the achievement of a mutually-acceptable modus-vivendi based on a shared perception of the perils involved in the current conflicts.

Originally published in The Hague Journal of Diplomacy, January 12,

2022

Diplomacy and Intercultural Communication

L et us go back to the year 1969. The then United States President, Richard Nixon, held a meeting with the then Japanese Prime Minister, Eisaku Sato. One of the problems besetting US-Japanese relations at that time had to do with the bilateral commercial relations between the two countries. To put it in simple terms: Japan was exporting considerably more to the US than it was importing from it. So, President Nixon asked Prime Minister Sato to adopt a pro-active policy aimed at reducing Japanese exports and increasing US imports. Sato replied: "*ZENSHO SHIMASU*," which literally means 'I will do my best.' Weeks and months elapsed and nothing happened. Nixon was furious. Didn't Sato say that he will do his best? Yes, he did. However, the question Nixon should have asked himself was not what did Sato **say**, but what did he actually **mean**? The Japanese Prime Minister's answer was an evasive reply. In fact, it is a polite way of avoiding any commitment, preferred to the explicit negative, which is considered rude in Japanese culture.

This case reflects a fundamental problem that exists in intercultural communication, in general, and in international diplomacy, in particular: on the one hand, we have the **intention** of the person conveying the message, and on the other the **interpretation** of the person receiving it.

Sato intended to say no, without actually saying no or anything that might even resemble a negative reply, as this would have been deemed to be rude. Nixon, for his part, interpreted Sato's words literally, and wouldn't have accorded it any other meaning, deriving his interpretation from a different cultural setting.

Problems in intercultural communication may be reflected verbally as well as in non-verbal manifestations. The aforementioned case is, of course, an example of intercultural communication problems as manifested in verbal terms. There are numerous examples of such intercultural linguistic misunderstandings.

Let us dwell on an example of intercultural communication problems in international diplomacy as reflected in a non-verbal manner. Two years ago, Sweden appointed a new ambassador to Iran, Peter Tejler. The newly appointed ambassador presented his credentials to the then Iranian President, Mahmoud Ahmadinejad. Following the official presentation of credentials, Ahmadinejad invited the Swedish ambassador to sit down and have a chat. The conversation went well until the ambassador crossed his legs and thus showed the sole of his shoe to the Iranian President. Ahmadinejad and all those present in the meeting were stunned. They couldn't believe what they were seeing.

What happened?

In Muslim cultures showing the sole of one's shoe to someone is considered to be rude and offensive. In order to demonstrate how offended he was, the Iranian President decided, in response, to cross his legs and show the sole of his shoe to the ambassador....

This whole episode led to a mini-crisis in relations between the two countries; a mini crisis, to be sure, that was soon resolved, but could have been avoided had the ambassador been more aware of the cross-cultural dimensions of his mode of conduct.

Again, also with regard to non-verbal manifestations of intercultural communication, there are numerous examples, the case aforementioned being a particularly noteworthy one.

What is particularly interesting in this case is that it involves a professional diplomat. One would expect a professional diplomat to be singularly aware of culture-related sensitivities. After all, professional diplomats are taught to be adept at intercultural communication.

Well, to be sure, professional diplomats **ought** to be more aware than others about the problems that might emerge in intercultural communication, and to be able to overcome them if necessary. That, of course, does not mean that they always **are**. Even professional diplomats, as we have seen in the case of the newly appointed Swedish ambassador to Iran, can fail in this regard.

This leads us to dwell on what we can call professional sub-cultures. The chances of intercultural communication problems between two individuals sharing the same profession would most probably be more limited than if the two didn't share the same profession. Thus, a mechanical engineer from the United States and a professional colleague from, let us say, Pakistan, would be unlikely to face the same risks of intercultural communication hurdles as two individuals from the same countries who do not share the same profession.

Why?

Because, even though they each belong to a different culture, the profession they share assures them a basic common denominator, a similar professional language, so to speak. Certainly, this will not be enough to prevent problems emerging which derive from a distinct cultural background. A shared sub-culture **limits** the chances of intercultural communication problems. It does not **prevent** them altogether.

Following the same logic, the sub-culture of diplomats should ensure that the chances of intercultural communication problems are even more limited. After all, as aforementioned, professional diplomats are actually taught to deal with people from other cultures. Intercultural communication is a central feature of their profession. However, even in the case of professional diplomats, a shared sub-culture can only **limit** the chances of intercultural communication problems. It does not **completely prevent** them.

In this context, we should be careful to distinguish between a sub-culture of diplomats and a sub-culture of diplomacy.

What's the difference between the two?

When we refer to **diplomats** we mean all those who serve in the diplomatic corps. They can be career diplomats or politically-appointed ones. Both, also under international law, would be defined as diplomats.

However, when we speak of **diplomacy** our range of reference broadens beyond the term **diplomats.**

Why?

Well, let us go back to the example we dwelt upon above regarding the meeting between President Nixon and Prime Miniser Sato. Both were involved in **diplomacy**, but neither was **a diplomat.** They were both politicians; yes, engaged in **diplomacy** at the highest level, but that did not turn them into **diplomats**.

That's why when we speak of a sub-culture of diplomacy, particularly in the context of intercultural communication, we should be aware that it encompasses – at least – both diplomats and politicians. Thus, the chances of problems emerging due to cultural differences might be even greater in a sub-culture of **diplomacy** than in a sub-culture of **diplomats.**

Certainly, diplomats can serve as facilitators in intercultural communication by clarifying and explaining – and here we go back to the beginning of the article – the **intention** of one party to another so as to avoid as far as possible any mistaken **interpretation**.

Glenn Fischer, a former US diplomat, who has devoted his time to studying this topic, has said, based both on his diplomatic experience and academic studies, that the greater the cultural differences of the parties involved in a diplomatic dialogue, the greater the risks of intercultural communication problems.

Professor Raymond Cohen, one of the foremost experts on this topic, wrote that US diplomats who have served in countries such as Britain, France or Germany tend to stress problems arising from intercultural communication to a considerably lesser extent than diplomats who have served in countries such as Iraq, Afghanistan or China. In other words, the wider the cultural gap of the country a US diplomat has served in with the United States, the greater the stress he or she would place on problems in intercultural communication in diplomacy.

We should stress a conceptual truth about culture which forms the basis of any discussion on intercultural communication: Culture is an attribute of a society that is transmitted to an individual by a process of socialization and acculturation. In other words, when we talk about culture, we refer to a characteristic of a society. We can talk of a Japanese or a Spanish culture. The individual does not possess a distinctive culture of his/her own, but the culture of the society to which he/she belongs.

Finally, a comment about humour and intercultural communication in international diplomacy:

Philip Habib, who served in high-ranking posts in the US State Department, has said that, based on his own diplomatic experience, and contrary to what is widely believed, humour can actually serve as a bridge between different cultures.

He relates how a Japanese audience would burst into laughter at hearing a typically "American" joke, notwithstanding the prevailing gaps between the two cultures. Humour, even a culturally-rooted one, can thus **facilitate** international diplomacy.

This is certainly a remarkable, indeed encouraging, finding that ought to make us aware not only of the problems besetting intercultural communication in diplomacy, but also of the means in facilitating it.

Originally published in American Diplomacy, September 2015.

Chapter 4

International Law and Diplomacy

Neither Cynical nor Dogmatic – The Right Attitude to International Law

Public International Law (henceforward referred to as International Law) tends to elicit from many people a cynical response; from many others a dogmatic attitude. International Law is thus seen by the first as irrelevant and unrealistic and by the latter as deserving a religious-like adoration.

Neither position is warranted by reality.

International Law affects all of us. There is hardly a domain of daily life that is not touched by it. From telecommunications to aviation, from agriculture to commerce, international law is almost everywhere. Unless one lives in a cave, in a remote area of the world, having scant contact with the outside world, the chances of not being affected by the workings of international law are almost non-existent.

Diplomatic relations between states are ruled by international law. Consulates which issue visas and passports do so according to multilateral or bilateral treaties. Sovereignty on land and in the seas is established by, and ruled according to, international law, which also delineates the legal framework of war and peace.

To be sure, there are instances in which countries violate international law. However, that by itself is no proof that international law is no law. After all, individuals violate domestic, municipal law. Does it mean that municipal law is no law?

Certainly, international law cannot be enforced in the same manner as municipal law can. A lot has been written about it. No intellectual gymnastics can close that gap. Enforcing international law is, at best, problematic when there is no consent; and it becomes very difficult when dealing with a powerful actor bent on pursuing its objective notwithstanding any outside legal constraint.

Further, international organizations may on occasion be comprised of violators of international law and thus be hardly in a moral position to ask others to abide by their rulings. Coalitions of countries not known for their respect for the rule of law, or having a particular political agenda, may attempt to enforce their views on the international community. All this does not contribute to enhancing the image of international law. Indeed, it leads many people to adopt a cynical attitude towards it.

Also, as some experts in international law have already stated, when faced with a stark choice between pursuing what they perceive to be their vital national interests or abiding by international law, states would most often than not choose the first over the latter.

However, it must be stressed that even when such

a choice is made decision-makers, particularly in liberal democracies, try to get legal advice in order to explain or even justify their actions on the basis of international law. Indeed, the political weight of international law can be gauged from the fact that foreign and defence policies are hardly decided upon without prior legal advice.

International law relies mostly on consent. Outside pressure can be brought to bear in order to achieve consent if that is not willingly available. On occasion, the international community can unite in order to enforce consent by force. Still, enforcement as such is more complex than it is under municipal law. That's why it is so important to see to it that international law is perceived to be not only relevant and useful but also just and equitable; a difficult task, to be sure.

It should be emphasized: most countries, most of the time, do not violate international law. Considering the complexities in enforcing international law, it is an impressive achievement.

Originally published in The New Jurist, January 10, 2013

Seventy Years to the UN Partition Plan for Palestine. What Happened and What Might Have Happened

On the 29th of November 1947, the General Assembly of the United Nations endorsed a partition plan entailing the establishment of a Jewish state and an Arab state in what was then Mandatory Palestine.

The Arab leaders rejected the plan as they were opposed to the establishment of a Jewish state in any part of Mandatory Palestine. The Jewish leaders, notwithstanding their reservations, decided to accept it. As a result, a series of attacks by Palestinian Arabs against the Jewish population evolved into a major military confrontation between the two sides.

Following the declaration of independence by David Ben-Gurion, who was to become the first Prime Minister of Israel, the surrounding Arab states joined the Palestinian Arabs in a war aimed at thwarting the establishment of the State of Israel.

The war ended in 1949, with heavy casualties on both sides. One percent of the Jewish population in Palestine in those years, i.e. around six thousand people, died during the war.

The Armistice Lines agreed upon by Israel and its Arab neighbours left the newly established Jewish state in control of a larger portion of territory than originally allotted to it by the UN partition plan, including the western part of Jerusalem, which would remain divided with Jordan until the end of the Six Day War in June 1967.

Few are the cases in history in which a counterfactual question can be answered, supposedly, so easily as in the case of the 1947 UN Partition Plan. What might have happened if the leadership of the Palestinian Arabs and the Arab States had accepted the UN Partition Plan?

Probably, there might have been no war, no bereavement, no refugees and thus no Nakba in 1947–1949. Perhaps, there might have been no Arab-Israeli wars in 1956, 1967, 1973…

How many lives might have been spared? How many wounded and disabled might have pursued a life without physical and emotional impediments?

Of course, one could imagine a scenario whereby the Arab side might have accepted the principle of partition, but not the particular map voted upon at the UN General Assembly.

Certainly, endorsing the principle of partition might have been pragmatically convenient for the Arab leadership in order to try to dilute the effects of the UN Partition Plan. Rather than thwart it militarily, they might have prevented its implementation diplomatically. They might have played for time by saying "Yes, but."

An alternative scenario founded on a logical historical process might have led to the creation of two states without the bloodshed and suffering entailed in the events as they unfolded from 1947 onwards.

However, one should bear in mind that for that to have happened there should have been an Arab leadership with foresight that eschewed political triumphalism and diplomatic rigidity.

The Arab leadership then was sincerely opposed to the establishment of a Jewish state in any part of Mandatory Palestine, no matter how big or small that state might have been. In addition, there was a widely-held belief that numbers and weapons would win the day: The Palestinian Arabs, assisted by the conventional armies of the Arab States, were expected to eradicate the organized Jewish presence in Mandatory Palestine and with it dash any hope of a Jewish state.

Therefore, one must distinguish between a depiction of a coherent counterfactual reality and the historical feasibility for that reality to take place considering all the variables known to us to have existed then. It is difficult to imagine a scenario different to what actually took place simply because of the mindset of the Arab leadership then.

A counterfactual question is indeed helpful in this case. Thanks to it we can imagine what might have happened if the Arab leaders had accepted the

UN Partition Plan. Thanks to it also, however, we can imagine how inconceivable that might have been considering the deep-seated attitudes prevailing then among those same Arab leaders.

The irony is that today most Arab leaders, including the internationally recognized leadership of the Palestinian Arabs, profess they would be willing to accept the creation of a Palestinian Arab state which would be smaller in size than the one entailed in the 1947 UN Partition Plan.

A lost opportunity in history rarely affords a second chance to those responsible for it; and when it does, it's appeal may seem less glowing than the lost opportunity concerned.

Seventy years of warfare and bloodshed have produced a reality on the ground that Arab leaders in 1947 didn't dare imagine: a strong Jewish state, technologically advanced, militarily powerful and economically prosperous, as a tacit ally of the pragmatic Sunni Arab world.

Originally published in The New Jurist, November 28, 2017

Why was the Kellogg-Briand Pact of 1928 a Watershed in the Evolution of Public International Law?

By the Kellogg-Briand Pact, officially known as the General Treaty for Renunciation of War as an Instrument of National Policy, sixty-two countries, representing most of the sovereign states in the international system at the time, pledged themselves to renounce war as "an instrument of national policy in their relations with each other." The Kellogg-Briand Pact was initially signed in 1928 by fifteen countries.

The Kellogg-Briand Pact was seen by contemporaries as a milestone in the history of international relations. With hindsight, this article argues that it can also be deemed to be a turning point.

Historic pact

It all started in 1927 with a diplomatic initiative by France's Foreign Minister, Aristide Briand, who proposed to his United States counterpart, Frank B. Kellogg, to sign a bilateral agreement stipulating that neither country would resort to war with each other and that any dispute would be settled by peaceful means. Kellogg responded by suggesting that such an agreement should be expanded into a multilateral pact, involving other countries as well, which Briand consented to. What began as a French initiative directed at the United States, ended up as an international pact, finally signed by most sovereign states in the world.

This was to be the first time in which the international community, or at least an overwhelming majority of it, officially and publicly committed itself to renounce war as an instrument of state. The League of Nations, set up in the wake of World War I, had already delineated legal limits to the resort to war, but had not called on member states to renounce it altogether.

According to the League of Nations Covenant, a three-month transition period would have to elapse before member states involved in a dispute were to be allowed to resort to the use of force, and that only after first having exhausted non-violent means to solve it.

As the late Professor Wilhelm G. Grewe, a former West German diplomat and an expert in public international law, would put it in his comprehensive work *The Epochs of International Law*: "The abandonment of the sovereign right of war through the procedural provisions of the League of Nations Covenant would bring about a certain restriction and constriction of war and, through the 1928 Kellogg-Briand Pact, its moral and legal outlawry as well."

The Kellogg-Briand Pact was to wield a direct influence on the development of public international law. Its echo was to resound through the chambers of international diplomacy for many years to come.

The Stimson Doctrine, enunciated by the US Secretary of State, Henry Stimson, on 7 January 1932, following the Japanese invasion of Manchuria in 1931, which became an integral part of public international law, made it clear that the Japanese occupation of Manchuria would not be recognized as it resulted from an illegal act, contrary to the Kellogg-Briand Pact of 1928.

It was subsequently reinforced by a resolution of the Assembly of the League of Nations that League Members should not recognize any situation, treaty or agreement brought about by means contrary to the League's Covenant or the Kellogg-Briand Pact. This has evolved into the principle in public international law that "legal rights cannot derive from an illegal situation (Ex injuria jus non oritur)."

The Atlantic Charter, which was signed by US President Franklin D. Roosevelt and British Prime Minister, Winston Churchill, on 14 August 1941, and was to become the diplomatic and conceptual basis for the future establishment of the United Nations, stressed that both leaders "believe that all of the nations of the world for realistic as well as spiritual reasons must come to the abandonment of the use of force."

At a subsequent conference held in Washington D.C. on 1 January 1942, twenty-six governments then at war with the Axis Powers, declared their adherence to the principles of the Atlantic Charter, including the reference aforementioned on the use of force.

The United Nations Charter (Article 2, Paragraph 4) stipulates that "all Members shall refrain [...] from the threat or use of force against the territorial integrity or political independence of any state or in any other manner inconsistent with the Purposes of the United Nations."

To be sure, the UN Charter went beyond the Kellogg-Briand Pact as it referred not only to war, but also to all kinds of armed force, including the mere threat of its use.

Several signatories of the Kellogg-Briand Pact, including the United States and Britain, had presented diplomatic notes prior to the Pact's ratification, indicating that wars in self-defence would be deemed acceptable.

Controversial provisions

The question that could be posed, of course, is why was not the reference to wars of self-defence mentioned in the Pact itself?

Kellogg himself, who was awarded the Nobel Peace Prize in 1929, explained that the right of self-defence was obvious and that therefore there was no need to mention it explicitly in the Pact. The right of self-defence, he emphasized, "is inherent in every sovereign state and is implicit in every treaty." Furthermore, he went on to elaborate that the consequent need to define terms such as "self-defence" and "aggressor" would be almost impossible to achieve. "It is not in the interest of peace that a treaty should stipulate a juristic conception of self-defence, since it is far too easy for the unscrupulous to mould events to accord with an agreed definition." The Pact, Kellogg stressed, did not prohibit the right of the signatories to defend themselves with force if necessary.

The Kellogg-Briand Pact was criticized for not having proposed any enforcement mechanism to prevent its violation (see, for instance, Henry Kissinger, Diplomacy, Simon and Schuster, New York, p. 374). That criticism is problematic. No international treaty can be enforced if there is no willingness to enforce it. True, the Kellogg-Briand Pact did not indicate what might occur should any of the signatories violate its terms. No enforcement mechanism was included in it. However, even if a clause had been added indicating what might happen, and/or mentioning an enforcement mechanism, in case of violation, that would not have helped unless those responsible for implementing such a clause would have been willing to do so when the moment arose. The main problem in international relations is usually not the lack of means, but rather the lack of willingness, to enforce an agreement.

No enforcement mechanism would have worked to prevent Nazi Germany, Fascist Italy, and Imperial Japan, which were bound by the Kellogg Briand Pact, from launching unprovoked military attacks, which clearly contravened its provisions. The League of Nations Covenant, which contained in it a call for collective action against an aggressor, did not deter any of the three aforementioned countries. Adding a clause to the Kellogg-Briand Pact aimed at deterring a potential violator of its provisions by threatening explicitly with concrete action might not have been enough to prevent them from carrying out their intended military attacks.

The principal problem entailed in the Kellogg-Briand Pact was not the fact that there was no explicit threat included in it in case its terms were to be violated nor, for that matter, that it lacked an enforcement mechanism.

It might be argued that the Kellogg-Briand Pact was founded upon a supposedly naïve belief about human nature and the way international relations are conducted.

Were the architects of the Pact unaware of the frailties of human behaviour and the anarchic nature of the international system?

Kellogg did not seem to entertain any idealistic notion about the Pact and its immediate success. In his speech in Oslo, upon being awarded the Nobel Peace Prize, on 10 December 1929, Kellogg said that "It is not to be expected that human nature will change in a day; perhaps it is too much to expect that the age-old institution of war, which has, through the centuries, been recognized by international law as a sovereign right [...] will be at once abolished."

He went on to argue that peace "can only be accomplished by slowly building the bulwarks of peace as peoples and nations have slowly and laboriously built the foundations of individual liberty and representative government."

Kellogg stressed his message: "We must remember that it is difficult to abolish the century-old practices of nations in a day or in a year. Time must elapse to soften the animosities and deaden the fears of people."

Final remarks

The Kellogg-Briand Pact should be assessed in its historical context. It was formulated a decade, more or less, after the end of World War I and a decade, more or less, prior to the outbreak of World War II. It came in the wake of the Locarno Treaty of 1925, which re-integrated Germany into the international scene as a leading diplomatic actor. The Kellogg-Briand Pact emerged in the midst of the so-called

"Locarno Spirit" of reconciliation, which prevailed then in Europe.

For all its shortcomings, the Kellogg-Briand Pact ought to be seen for what it was, and for what it turned out to be: a watershed in international relations for the way it influenced the development of public international law and of diplomatic discourse. No legal analysis on the use of force in international relations can omit the Kellogg-Briand Pact as a landmark event. As Professor Malcolm Shaw wrote in *International Law*, "resort to force is not acceptable in international law, especially since the 1928 Kellogg-Briand Pact and article 2 (4) of the United Nations Charter."

Originally published in the Cambridge International Law Journal, April 26, 2021

The Right of Self-Determination: A Further Principle

The right of self-determination, which is central in international law, has been one of the most contentious issues in international relations since the Congress of Vienna in 1814–1815. The Versailles Treaty of 1919, following World War I, was ostensibly based, among other principles, on national self-determination, though critics have charged that it did not fully pursue the right of self-determination to its ultimate logic. Many people, like the Sudeten Germans, were not given the right to determine themselves freely, it is argued.

The post-World War II map was gradually delineated by the self-determination of the people who had been living under colonial rule; but the post-Cold War period is characterized by the fragmentation of previously constituted states into a diversified mosaic of independent states, as in the former Yugoslavia and Soviet Union. Indeed, among the bloodiest conflicts in recent years those related to the former Yugoslavia, and the application of the right of self-determination within it, emerge as the most prominent.

The principle of self-determination is deemed to be a right under international law. Peoples under colonial rule or foreign occupation are granted a right to determine for themselves the sovereignty under which they wish to live. A region within an already existing sovereign state is not granted the same right. The secession of a certain area from the independent state to which it belongs is legal only so long as there is a mutual consent by the people inhabiting the area concerned and the central government of the state. An example that springs to mind is the agreed separation of the Czech and Slovak people into two separate states. To be sure, international law does conceive the possibility of a region seceding from the sovereign state to which it belongs even if the central government is opposed to such a move, in extreme circumstances. The application of the right of self-determination in the case of Kosovo is a contentious example of that.

Implementing Self-Determination

Certainly, the right of self-determination may be applied in such a manner that does not necessarily manifest itself in the form of an independent state, but rather of an autonomous area, such as Catalonia in Spain and Quebec in Canada.

The question we wish to raise is as follows: should the right of self-determination be implemented in the same manner for a people having no state of their own as for a people having already such a state? Should the implementation of that right be exclusively territorial in nature or embrace the notion of nationhood in a broader sense?

For instance, should the right of self-determination of the Albanians in Kosovo bear the same legal weight as that of the Slovenians, bearing in mind that the Albanian people have already a state of their own whilst the Slovenian people did not?

Indeed, in the case of Kosovo, the Albanian population sees itself as being ethnically part of the Albanian people living within the sovereign territory of Albania. There is no distinct sense of identity. To claim that the Albanian nation has no sovereign state of its own would be incorrect.

Thus, considering the aforementioned, the answer to the question we pose would be: The Albanian people have already a state of their own. The future of Kosovo's Albanian population would have to be settled not merely on the basis of the application of the right of self-determination as it is construed at present, but rather following the principle that such a right, in this case, does not have to be fulfilled necessarily through the establishment of an independent state.

The principle we propose adds a further dimension to the right of self-determination. We do not wish to argue against the right as such, but in favor of a further principle underpinning that right.

Palestinian Case

A similar case, though rather more complex, is that of the Palestinian Arabs. Being part of the Arab nation as a whole, it may be argued that, with more than 20 sovereign states already in existence, the Arab people have already fulfilled their right to self-determination through the establishment of several independent states. Indeed, bearing in mind that Jordan, formerly part of Mandatory Palestine, has a population comprising more than 70% Palestinian Arabs, the right of self-determination has already been fulfilled as applied to the Palestinian Arabs as well.

The question that emerges in this context is whether the Arab nation has a sense of unity which would justify such an argument.

The answer is clearly not simple.

Institutionally, the Arab states have followed, in some instances, a path indicating a common origin and, indeed, a shared destiny. The Arab League is one such example. Furthermore, the Arabs share the same language; and the overwhelming majority of them adhere to the same religion. They convey a sense of common heritage which, at least ostensibly, binds them together.

However, the Arab world has been beset by internal struggles. These have been caused by political differences, but these differences hardly negate the existence of an Arab nation.

Palestinian nationalism has been shaped particularly since 1967 into a distinctive political phenomenon. It may be argued that the Palestinian Arabs have a separate identity which they wish to foster, though it would be naïve to believe that such a separate identity negates their being an integral part of the Arab people.

Thus, looking at it from a wider Arab perspective, and according to the principle we wish to propose, the Palestinian Arabs' right to self-determination might be constrained in its application by the fact that there are more than 20 Arab states already in existence.

On the other hand, assessing the question from a narrower angle, it might be said that the distinctive national character of the different entities comprising the Arab world is much stronger than the comprehensive Arab identity. In that case, the question to be asked is not necessarily if there are any other Arab states, but rather if there are any other Palestinian states.

It is difficult to determine whether the first or the latter argument should be applied in the case of the Palestinian Arabs. Both are equally legitimate and persuasive, though the first tends to be thematically more suitable to the principle advanced in this article.

Taiwan Case

The case of Taiwan is, no doubt, an interesting one in this context. To recognize the right of self-determination of the population of Taiwan might be construed – certainly by China – as illegal, bearing in mind that the territory might be deemed to have seceded from mainland China.

The Nationalists in Taiwan traditionally argued that they were the legitimate government of the whole of China. Their aim was not ostensibly to create a separate Chinese state. The argument revolved around the legitimacy of the Communist government in mainland China versus that of the Nationalist, having its situ in the island of Taiwan. However, an increasing number of people in Taiwan have called for the independence of the island. China is adamantly opposed to such a move, considering the island an integral part of its sovereign territory.

How would the principle we propose apply in this case?

Even if under international law a unilateral declaration of independence by Taiwan were not deemed to be an act of secession, the question that would emerge in the context of our discussion is whether the fact that there is a Chinese state already in existence should be taken into consideration in assessing the limits of the right of self-determination of the island of Taiwan?

The people of Taiwan might argue that, with the Communist regime in control over mainland China, they cannot see themselves as being part of China and wish to live under a differently constituted political regime, something impossible to achieve within the sovereign territory of China.

Such a stance is based on what is known as "internal self-determination," i.e., the freedom to select the political regime under which a people wishes to live, rather than "external self-determination," i.e., the right to determine the sovereign authority that should rule over the people concerned.

The people of Taiwan may not necessarily object to being part of China as a country, but to being part of a regime in China that is alien to their traditions and wishes.

Sudeten German Case

To go back in time, should the principle of self-determination have been implemented in the case of the Sudeten Germans, living in a region that was part of the sovereign territory of Czechoslovakia, in the same manner as that of the Czechs, considering that the German people had already a state of their own and the Czechs did not? To be sure, in the case of the Sudeten Germans, their preference was to be incorporated into Germany, rather than become an independent state, but that was to be done at the expense of Czechoslovakia and its vital security interests, whilst the latter was willing to extend the autonomy of the German inhabitants in the region.

The case of the Sudeten Germans (and, to a lesser extent, of the Albanians in Kosovo) raises a further question: Should the unhindered right of self-determination be applied also when the exercise of such a right might endanger the sovereignty of an already established state?

The question raised here is not predicated on the notion that the right of self-determination should not be legally binding under international law. Rather, the aim is to broaden the conceptual definition of the term so as to apply it in a manner that is both just and feasible.

The fact that a nation state X exists does not negate the right of people X, living elsewhere, to exercise their right of self-determination. The question is whether such a right should be extended to include the creation of an additional X state? Indeed, whether the fact that such a state X already exists may not limit the scope of the self-determination of people X living elsewhere?

What is proposed here is to add a further principle upon which the right of self-determination ought to be founded under international law, and to define the conceptual framework of this legal right so as to include the question: Has this right been exercised already by this nation anywhere within the international system, and if so how?

Originally published in American Diplomacy, January 13, 2012

A Conceptual Framework of Analysis to Interpret United Nations Security Council Resolution 242

Resolution 242 was adopted in the wake of the Six Day War of June 1967, during which Israel captured the Sinai Peninsula and the Gaza Strip from Egypt, the West Bank (Judea and Samaria) and East Jerusalem from Jordan and the Golan Heights from Syria.

Every peace agreement between Israel and its Arab neighbors makes direct and explicit reference to Resolution 242 as the legal cornerstone upon which it is based.

The Camp David Accords between Israel and Egypt of September 1978 and the Peace Agreement signed by both countries in March 1979 were founded on Resolution 242; which was also mentioned as the basis for the Oslo Accords between Israel and the Palestinian Liberation Organization (P.L.O.) of September 1993. Resolution 242 was referred to as the legal basis of the peace agreement which was signed by Israel and Jordan in October 1994.

Resolution 242 is the only United Nations Security Council resolution on the pacific resolution of the Arab-Israeli conflict which has been accepted by both Israel and its Arab neighbors.

Israel, Egypt and Jordan endorsed Resolution 242 already in November 1967. Syria refused to follow suit until 1973. Following the Yom Kippur War of October 1973, the Syrians adopted United Nations Security Council Resolution 338, which called on the warring sides to negotiate peace on the basis of UN Security Council Resolution 242, thus endorsing it as the basis for peace.

Indeed, UN Security Council Resolution 338 is usually mentioned in official documents alongside UN Security Council Resolution 242 as the basis for peace between Israel and its Arab neighbors.

The PLO refused, for many years, to endorse Resolution 242 as it did not make any explicit reference to the Palestinian Arabs as a separate entity.

To be sure, there is a general reference in Resolution 242 to "achieving a just settlement of the refugee problem," which may be interpreted as alluding to Palestinian Arab refugees (as well as to Jewish refugees from Arab countries). However, apart from that, the Palestinian Arabs as a separate factor in the conflict are not specifically mentioned in Resolution 242.

Still, as already mentioned, the Oslo Accords between Israel and the PLO were based on Resolution 242. Thus, the PLO and the Palestinian Authority, which was established in the wake of the Oslo Accords of September 1993, have recognized Resolution 242 as a basis for peace.

UN Security Council Resolution 242 was not adopted under Chapter VII of the United Nations Charter, which would have been unequivocally binding, having been adopted in the light of a situation deemed to be a "threat to the peace, breaches of the peace and acts of aggression." Resolution 242 was endorsed under Chapter VI of the UN charter, which obtains in cases related to the "pacific resolution of disputes." However, having been adopted by both sides to the conflict it could be said to be binding, albeit in a consensual, rather than an enforced, manner.

It should be noted that, although UN Security Council Resolution 242 has been accepted by both sides to the Arab-Israeli conflict, Israel and its Arab neighbors have accorded it a different interpretation.

For instance, Resolution 242 calls on Israeli armed forces to withdraw "from territories occupied in the recent conflict."

The Arab side has consistently argued that Israel was obliged under the terms of Resolution 242 to withdraw completely to the lines prevailing prior to the outbreak of the Six Day War of June 1967. In other words, according to this interpretation, Israel must return to the territorial status quo ante.

Israel, on the other hand, has contended that Resolution 242 speaks for itself. Israel is not requested to withdraw from all the territories, but from "territories." The absence of the article 'the' or of the word 'all' preceding the term "territories" is not accidental, but a clear allusion to the fact that the drafters foresaw a withdrawal of Israeli armed forces to an unspecified line that might be different from the one existing prior to the Six Day War. There was certainly no obligation to withdraw fully to the boundaries existing before the War, which, anyway, were Armistice Lines and not final and mutually-agreed borders.

This particular phrase has been a bone of contention between the two sides, occupying some brilliant legal minds in an earnest endeavor at persuading the other of the rightness of its own interpretation.

A further interpretative dispute between the Israelis and the Arabs and their respective supporters for many a year has been over whether Resolution 242 calls on Israel to withdraw unilaterally or only in the framework of a peace agreement with its Arab neighbors.

Indeed, the Arab side and many a political and legal commentator siding with it have protested that Israel does not implement United Nations resolutions, alluding in this regard first and foremost to UN Security Council Resolution 242.

According to their line of reasoning, Israel should have withdrawn completely from the territories it had captured during the Six Day War, in the same manner, for example, that Iraq was requested to withdraw from Kuwait following the invasion of the latter by the first in August 1990. Israel has been treated differently than other countries that violate United Nations resolutions, so it has been argued.

The counter argument advanced to refute this dwells on the difference between a United Nations Security Council resolution which requests a country to withdraw unilaterally, i.e., Iraq with reference to Kuwait, and one that calls on it to withdraw in the context of a peace agreement, following negotiations between the warring sides, i.e. Israel as regards the territories it captured during the Six Day War.

Also, it has been contended, Israel captured those territories in a war of self-defence against countries calling for its destruction and undertaking aggressive and illegal actions against it. Iraq invaded Kuwait without being under any threat of attack by the latter, let alone being menaced with physical extinction.

There is a legal difference, according to this counter-argument, espoused among others by the Cambridge University scholar Sir Elihu Lauterpacht, between unlawful territorial change by an aggressor and lawful territorial change in response to an aggressor. Of course, the Arab side has contended that Israel was the aggressor in the Six Day War, and thus any territorial change in its favor would be ipso facto illegal.

Considering the discrepancies with regard to the correct way to interpret UN Security Council

Resolution 242, a conceptual framework of analysis is proposed here in order to establish a structured system for its interpretation.

This conceptual framework of analysis is based on the legal classifications and terms of reference that define the interpretations accorded to the United States Constitution by legal scholars and Supreme Court judges.

We propose, therefore, to interpret UN Security Council Resolution 242 according to one or more of the three following conceptual terms:

- The intentional version [Original Intent], looking at the intention of those who drafted Resolution 242;
- The literal version [Textualism], confined to an analysis of what is written in Resolution 242;
- The evolutionary version [Living Tree], which interprets Resolution 242 according to changing circumstances.

According to the intentional version [Original Intent], one would look for evidence regarding the original intention of those who drafted Resolution 242, in this case US and British politicians and diplomats, as the resolution was drafted by both delegations to the UN and presented to the Security Council by the British. To be sure, there are several written and oral testimonies of those involved in the drafting of Resolution 242. In this context, one could also follow the background, and the process leading to, the drafting of Resolution 242.

For example, those who argue that Resolution 242 does not oblige Israel to withdraw completely from all the territories captured during the Six Day War would refer to the words of Lord Caradon (Hugh Foot), the British Ambassador to the United Nations at the time of the drafting of Resolution 242 and one of its drafters, who subsequently said that the absence of the article "the" or the word "all" was intentional.

Further, the evidence of then US Ambassador to the United Nations, Arthur Goldberg, who was involved in the drafting of Resolution 242, that stressed that it was drafted the way it was on purpose. According to Ambassador Goldberg, Israel was not requested to withdraw fully to the lines existing prior to the Six Day War.

The fact that a Soviet-led effort at tabling a resolution calling on Israel to withdraw completely to the boundaries existing prior to the Six Day War was rejected by the United States and Britain, which instead put forward what was to be known as Resolution 242, may prove the existence of a diplomatic-legal process preceding the adoption of Resolution 242 which validates the interpretation that the drafters did not intend to call on Israel to withdraw fully to the lines prevailing before the Six Day War. The literal version [Textualism] would lead us to interpret Resolution 242 on the basis of what is written in it. The text itself and a literal interpretation of it would be of paramount importance in this context. One would confine oneself to what is written rather than to what might have been intended to be written.

On the one hand, this might lead to an interpretation according to which Israel is called to withdraw from territories and not from all of the territories, nor even from the territories, captured during the Six Day War.

On the other hand, the French version of Resolution 242 calls on Israel to withdraw from the territories ("des territories") and not just from territories, captured during the Six Day War.

Apart from English, French was also an official language at the United Nations at the time of the drafting of Resolution 242 and therefore the French text might be deemed to be equally valid to the English version.

In this regard, one would have to delve further into this and ask oneself which language should take legal precedence in this instance? Which of the two versions – the English or the French – would have the legal edge, so to speak, in order to determine which one has more legal weight than the other?

The Arab side and legal scholars adhering to an interpretation whereby Israel should withdraw completely from the territories captured during the

Six Day War might point out that Resolution 242 emphasizes "the inadmissibility of the acquisition of territory by war." The capture of any territory by Israel during the Six Day War could be deemed to be, according to this interpretation, inadmissible, thus foreclosing any legal right for Israel to retain territory beyond the lines existing prior to that War.

The Israeli side and legal scholars that find the aforementioned argument to be questionable, contend that the clause on "the inadmissibility of the acquisition of territory by war" is a general principle mentioned in the preamble of Resolution 242 and not in its operative clauses, in which Israel is called to withdraw "from territories," thus legally allowing a modification of the pre-existing lines.

Lastly, if an analysis based on the evolutionary version [Living Tree] is undertaken, then one would interpret Resolution 242 according to changing circumstances.

For instance, one could argue, on the one hand, that the fact that Israel withdrew from the Sinai Peninsula in the context of a peace agreement with Egypt and from parts of the West Bank as part of the Oslo Accord with the PLO that Resolution 242 has been accepted by both sides as entailing an Israeli withdrawal in the framework of a mutually-agreed treaty rather than as a result of a unilaterally binding call for withdrawal.

On the other hand, as a result of the Israeli withdrawal from the entire Sinai Peninsula, in accordance with the peace agreement between Israel and Egypt of March 1979, one could contend that a precedent has been established whereby Israel should withdraw completely to the lines existing prior to the Six Day War, albeit as a corollary of a peace agreement.

Furthermore, both Israel and the United States have argued that any peace agreement reached between Israel and the Palestinian Authority should take into account the changing demographic reality in the West Bank (Judea and Samaria), let alone in East Jerusalem.

Thus, most of the Israeli inhabitants residing beyond the lines prevailing previous to the Six Day War would have to remain under Israeli sovereignty in the case of East Jerusalem or be incorporated within Israeli sovereign territory in the case of some of the settlements in the West Bank (Judea and Samaria). This would inevitably entail some modifications in the boundaries from those existing prior to that War.

In this context, both Israel and the United States have mentioned the possibility of land swaps to compensate the Palestinian Authority for any loss of territory, something the Palestinian leadership has not ruled out in principle.

The examples aforementioned may not have been foreseen by the drafters of UN Security Council Resolution 242. The text of Resolution 242 does not necessarily account for the changing circumstances since it was first drafted in November 1967. Thus, an analysis of Resolution 242 that takes into account the changing demographic, territorial, diplomatic and legal realities would be undertaken as part of an evolutionary analysis [Living Tree].

The conceptual framework of analysis proposed in this article to interpret UN Security Council Resolution 242 is aimed at delineating a structured system for the study and legal interpretation of the most important resolution on Arab-Israeli peace that has ever been adopted by the United Nations Security Council. It may serve, as well, as a conceptual framework of analysis to help interpret other United Nations Security Council resolutions.

Originally published in The New Jurist, December 20, 2011

The Risk of Trivializing International Law

The appointment by the United Nations Human Rights Council of a special commission to investigate Israeli actions during the latest war in the Gaza Strip seems to confirm the skepticism with which that organization is held by many people in North America and Europe.

The UN Human Rights Council replaced in 2006 the UN Human Rights Commission. Unfortunately, the change in name was not followed by a change in attitude.

The obsessive concentration on Israel, at the expense of many other countries where human rights are flagrantly violated, is not the exclusive purview of the UN Human Rights Commission, to be sure. The UN in general tends to devote more time to Israel than to any other country; so much so that one wonders if Israel did not exist what would the UN do with so much spare time left.

The appointment of the special commission on the Gaza War is particularly odd.

To begin with, there is a clear assumption that only Israel's actions must be investigated.

Also, it presumes that Israel has infringed humanitarian international law before the commission has even started working.

Further, the person appointed to head the commission is Professor William Schabas, whose record is singularly hostile to Israel. Suffice it to look at his statements on Israel and its leaders to realize that. Even the notion of ostensible impartiality is clearly absent in his case. Let us be clear: Professor Schabas is not critical of Israel. He is completely biased against it.

Beyond that, he is quoted as having said that Iran's call to destroy Israel is mere "political views" and not "a call for genocide." I always thought that calling for the destruction of a sovereign state, which is a member of the United Nations, is something that goes beyond "political views." Indeed, one wonders why an expert in international law would not be able to find a suitable legal term to define such a call to destroy Israel, even if he deemed the word "genocide" to be inappropriate.

Apart from that, Professor Schabas appears to have a problem connecting legal opinion with historical facts. When asked on the 12th of August on Israeli TV (Channel 10) why did he call to bring Benjamin Netanyahu to justice at the International Criminal Court, he replied that his comment was advanced in relation to the Goldstone Commission. His remark, he stressed, should be viewed in the context of that Commission. The Goldstone Commission was set up, following Operation Cast Lead in 2008, to investigate Israeli actions in Gaza. The problem with his remark, though, is that Netanyahu was then Leader of the Opposition, and his name wasn't even mentioned in the Goldstone Commission.

Thus, to appoint a person who is clearly biased against Israel, who believes that a call to destroy a sovereign state should be regarded solely as "political views" and who justifies his legal opinion to bring an Israeli political leader to justice based on mistaken facts, if not on his fertile imagination, is incomprehensible.

Israel's legendary foreign minister, the late Abba Eban, once said that if a resolution were presented by countries hostile to Israel before the UN stipulating that the Earth was flat, only a minority of countries would oppose it.

International Law is too important to be left in the hands of institutions that make a mockery out of it. If international law is to be taken seriously, it must be formulated, interpreted and implemented seriously. The UN is engaged in various laudable enterprises. However, the UN, and particularly the UN Human Rights Council, runs the risk of trivializing international law. That would be even worse than having no legal framework within which international relations are conducted.

Originally published in The New Jurist, August 14, 2014

The Status of Jerusalem: A Matter of Logic

Few are the cases in which the international community
has ignored reality and worked against its own declared
policy as in the case of Jerusalem.

Yoav J. Tenembaum

The status of Jerusalem as Israel's capital has
become one of the greatest make-believe issues
in the history of international relations. Few are the
cases in which the international community has
ignored reality and worked against its own declared
policy as in the case of Jerusalem.

Certainly there are occasions in international
relations in which a modicum of make-believe is
necessary to ameliorate conflicts and prevent crises.
However, in this case, the degree and persistence of
make-believe is quite singular.

The official stance of the international community
is that a future peace agreement between Israel
and the Palestinian Arabs ought to be based on
the boundaries prevailing prior to the Six Day War
in June 1967, which included west Jerusalem as an
integral part of Israel.

Further, the official position of the Palestinian
Authority is that east Jerusalem should become the
capital of a future Palestinian state.

If that is so, what is the problem of at least west

Jerusalem being recognized as Israel's capital? Indeed, why shouldn't the embassies of all the countries that recognize Israel be located in west Jerusalem? The argument adduced by the governments of many states, particularly in Europe, is that such a move might be possible following a peace agreement between Israel and the Palestinian Arabs.

That, of course, is a legitimate argument, but it contradicts the official position of those same governments as west Jerusalem would remain under Israeli control following a peace agreement, even according to the PA.

If west Jerusalem is not recognized as part of Israeli sovereign territory, and thus is not allowed to be Israel's capital, when all the maps of a future peace agreement entail the continued control by Israel of at least west Jerusalem, why on earth accept any other part of pre-1967 Israel as sovereign Israeli territory? What is the difference then between, say, Tel Aviv, Haifa, Beersheba and west Jerusalem? The boundaries existing before the outbreak of the Six Day War included the four aforementioned cities as part of Israeli sovereign territory.

Israel is a unique case in international law. According to the international community it has no capital. The embassies are located in Tel Aviv while the Israeli government, parliament and the Supreme Court are located in west Jerusalem.

The argument according to which an international

recognition of at least west Jerusalem as Israel's capital might produce an adverse effect in the Arab and Muslim world is understandable, though illogical.

As mentioned before, even the PA, and with it the Arab countries, claims that a future peace agreement would have to be based on the June 1967 borders. Thus, according to the official Arab position, west Jerusalem, at least, would remain under Israeli control.

Why wait for a final peace agreement in the case of west Jerusalem, and not in the case of any other city in Israel? This is not a matter of ideology, but of logic.

The time has come to eschew fictional solutions and imaginary realities and start recognizing what the international community claims it does anyway – that at least west Jerusalem is an integral part of Israeli sovereign territory and will remain so even following a peace agreement.

Originally published in The Jerusalem Post, January 3, 2018

Forty Years to the Zionism Equals Racism Resolution

Forty years ago this year, the General Assembly of the United Nations (UN) adopted a resolution equating Zionism with racism and racial discrimination.

Resolution 3379, which was adopted on November 10, 1975, stipulated that "Zionism is a form of racism and racial discrimination." Seventy-two countries voted in favor of the resolution, thirty-five were against, and thirty-two abstained.

Although General Assembly resolutions are usually not legally binding, their influence on the development of public international law can be significant, as Professor Malcolm Shaw has stressed in his best-seller book International Law. Further, their political echo may resound more loudly in the realm of international diplomacy than many a legally-binding resolution.

A memorable image of that day has remained rooted in the collective consciousness of Israelis: that of Israel's ambassador at the United Nations, Haim Herzog (who was subsequently to become President of Israel), tearing the resolution in half as he concluded his speech at the General Assembly of the UN. His speech, alongside that of the United

States Ambassador, Daniel Patrick Moynihan, is recalled by many contemporaries as memorable also for its rhetorical power and analytical rigor.

The resolution caused a profound effect not only in Israel and among Jews worldwide, but also among many people in democratic countries. The name of streets in Israel bearing the name of the United Nations was changed into Zionism. In the United States, citizens bore buttons on their lapels saying, "I am a Zionist."

Mexico, which had voted in favor of the resolution, was ostracized by many in the United States who refused to visit the country.

The uproar caused by the resolution went well beyond the realms of diplomacy. The automatic coalition of Communist, Arab, and third world countries, which passed the resolution produced on this occasion an unprecedented scenario of disgust among many people in the democratic world, who thought that the United Nations had gone beyond the pale.

Instead of being a legal framework and diplomatic arena aimed at ameliorating conflicts and enhancing international understanding, the United Nations became the focus of sharp discord and deep animosity. Its prestige as an international institution had reached its lowest ebb. A phenomenon that would recur in subsequent years had become an integral part of its institutional personality: a combination of authoritarian and totalitarian states had taken hold of its agenda in a futile attempt to distort history and spread hatred.

A simple truth became abundantly clear: without a reputation for fair and equitable debate and adjudication, the United Nations had precious little chance of being perceived as a respectable international institution. The image of the United Nations as an international legal setting within which justice could be imparted was seriously tarnished. The tendency to settle international disputes beyond the realm of its authority was enhanced.

The United Nations, which should have conveyed a message of mutual respect and reconciliation, was suddenly identified with bigotry and discrimination.

It should be stressed: The General Assembly did not pass a resolution that could be construed as being merely hostile to Israel. The resolution it adopted equated Zionism, the national liberation movement of the Jewish people, with racism and racial discrimination, an unprecedented step. After all, it was the United Nations that had called for the creation of a Jewish state on November 29, 1947 (General Assembly Resolution 181). Israel was admitted subsequently as a full-fledged member of the United Nations on May 11, 1949 (General Assembly Resolution 273).

Israel was thus not only a geographical reality in situ, but a legal entity recognized in international law as an equal member of the family of nations. To equate Zionism with racism and racial discrimination was tantamount to claiming that Israel's raison d'etre was illegitimate. This was not only morally unacceptable but legally incoherent.

Zionism was thus singled out, the same way Jews had been throughout history. That was the way it was seen, not only by Israel and Jews worldwide, but by the United States. As Moynihan, the US Ambassador to the UN said, "The abomination of anti-Semitism has been given international sanction. The General Assembly today grants symbolic amnesty – and more – to the murderers of the six million European Jews." He went on to stress that "A great evil has been loosed upon the world." He was expressing the views of many non-Jews all over the world.

The Italian newspaper La Stampa called the resolution "An Anti-Semitic Verdict."

The British newspaper The Daily Telegraph's editorial headline read: "UNO's Racist Orgy."

The French newspaper L'Aurore went so far as to claim that "For men of good will the UN has ceased to exist yesterday, at 2.38 GMT."

Even the British newspaper The Guardian, known for its critical stance towards Israel, declared that "many of the countries which provide the automatic majority on these occasions are up to their knees in racial and tribal ambiguities, but without having a democratic apparatus such as Israel's."

At the end of the Cold War, the United Nations General Assembly revoked its Zionism equals racism and racial discrimination resolution. On December 16, 1991, it adopted resolution 46/86 revoking resolution 3379 by a majority of 111 to 25 with 13 abstentions. It took sixteen years, and a changed international landscape, for the United Nations to amend its ways.

US President George H.W. Bush introduced the aforementioned resolution, stressing that "to equate Zionism with racism is to reject Israel itself, a member of good standing in the United Nations." He went on to state the obvious: "This body cannot claim to seek peace and at the same time challenge Israel's right to exist."

Conclusion

The Zionism is Racism Resolution adopted by the UN General Assembly forty years ago this year was a corollary of historical circumstances. The Cold War had produced a large coalition of Communist countries, as well as Arab and third world states that could muster a plurality of votes at international organizations against Israel. On this occasion, the resolution clearly and explicitly questioned the legitimacy of Israel by equating Zionism with racism and racial discrimination. However, it would be a mistake to see this as merely a historically-contingent event, for Israel and Zionism have been the focus of a particularly hostile attention at international forums since then, as well.

Thus, although singular in its content and effects, the Zionism is Racism Resolution reflects, in a sense, an ongoing obsession with Israel at the UN to this day. The effect of that is not only detrimental to Israel's image, but also to the reputation of the UN as a fair and balanced institution. Indeed, one of the main characteristics of a just legal system is its unbiased modus operandi. This was hardly reflected in the Zionism is Racism Resolution. To be sure, the problem entailed in directing so much venom on Israel and everything it represents is that international law might be seen as a prescriptive framework for the conduct of international relations, but not as an actual legal setting meriting respect. The lesson to be derived from the Zionism is Racism Resolution is as pertinent today as it was forty years ago when it was adopted.

Originally published in Travaux: The Berkley Journal of International Law Blog. Reproduced by History News Network, March 31, 2015

Two Conflicting Legal Principles – The Argentinean Diplomatic Campaign Regarding the Falklands-Malvinas Islands

Almost thirty years to the Argentinean invasion of the Falklands/Malvinas Islands and the conflict is once again in the headlines. Although not violent, the current dispute has assumed a confrontational rhetorical character not seen since the Argentinean invasion of the Islands on the 2nd of April, 1982.

Whereas every democratically-elected government in Argentina since 1983 has continued to claim sovereignty over the Islands, it is the current administration of President Cristina Kirchner that has elevated its claim into an active diplomatic campaign.

This diplomatic campaign has coincided with the announcement that drilling for oil in the area of the Islands would commence. The prospect of the discovery of oil and the revenues that might accrue would not have left any government in Argentina apathetic; nor, for that matter, would it have left any government in Britain apathetic. Of course, the stance adopted by Argentina is not just pragmatic in nature, prompted exclusively by economic motives. There is a genuine national consensus in Argentina about the Malvinas. I can recall, as a child, being taught in school that the Malvinas were an integral part of Argentina. Indeed, the Islands figured prominently in any map of Argentina shown to us in school as part of the sovereign territory of the country.

The current diplomatic campaign conducted by Argentina, though, seems to be linked to the possible discovery of precious natural resources in the Islands and their adjacent areas, and is not merely a reflection of an understandable legal claim of sovereignty.

Also, to be sure, being a cause that unites almost all Argentineans, the Malvinas can distract public opinion from domestic problems and internal divisions. In this context, it is interesting to note that even such a prestigious newspaper as La Nacion, known for its consistent criticism of the Kirchner Administration, has come out in favour of its diplomatic campaign. Thus, politically this campaign has already reaped fruits.

Further, diplomatically Argentina has managed to enlist Latin American countries to its cause. So much so, that even some of Argentina's neigbours (including land-locked Paraguay) have declared that no ship bearing the Falklands Islands flag would be permitted to anchor in any of their ports.

In this regard, Argentina's rhetoric seems to have been successful. The repeated negative references to Britain as a colonial power could not but have resonated in the collective Latin American consciousness so sensitive to the perils of colonialism.

The problem with this kind of rhetoric is that, in

a sense, it preaches to the converted. In other words, it is aimed at persuading those that didn't need to be persuaded.

Further, it has led to a display of overconfidence on the part of Argentina's government, leading it to urge at the latest conference of American countries meeting in Colombia to adopt an unequivocal pro-Argentinean stance regarding the Malvinas, which was politely rejected. References to the British as "pirates" and singularly critical allusions to their colonial past have hardly helped in this regard.

This kind of diplomatic campaign also leads the other side to the dispute, in this case Britain, to adopt a confrontational language in defence, not only of its cause, but of its national pride. Prime Minister David Cameron's retort that Argentina behaves in a colonial manner by wishing to impose its sovereignty on an unwilling population should be understood in this context.

No matter how solid its legal claim may be, Argentina's current campaign is in part disingenuous. The current government either does not even allude in its public statements to the military invasion of 1982 or just refers to it as a decision by an unelected Junta, totally unconnected to the current democratically-elected government.

What it omits to say is that the Peronist Party, an offspring of which currently rules in Argentina, openly and enthusiastically supported the decision to invade the Islands back then in 1982. To be fair, almost all political parties backed the decision.

This is a weak point, to say the least, which the Argentinean government cannot dismiss lightly or pretend it never happened.

After all, the nature of the dispute changed radically as a result of the invasion. What was until then a diplomatic/legal dispute, in which both sides were trying to find a mutually-agreed solution, suddenly became a violent confrontation, which resulted in a heightened sense of fear on the British side. Evidence of that can be found on the ground, on the Islands, where a strong British military force is ever ready to defend them.

To be sure, Britain's claim that only the right of self-determination of the local population should determine the status of the Islands, though politically sound, is legally questionable. After all, the United Nations has called on both sides to negotiate, something Britain has refused to do. Also, the matter of decolonization is clearly defined in international law, something that could back up Argentina's claim.

What makes this dispute rather sui generis is that two conflicting legal principles seem to be at stake: decolonization and self-determination. In the past, in cases where decolonization was concerned, the two were one and the same. In this case, they are not.

Originally published in The New Jurist, May 23, 2012

Chapter 5

Theory and History

Why Historians Need Imagination

There are two types of imagination: *Fantasy-directed imagination*, and *Reality-directed imagination*.

Fantasy-directed imagination is aimed at depicting a scenario that goes beyond reality. An example of *fantasy-directed imagination* would be the creation of Mickey Mouse. *Reality-directed imagination*, on the other hand, is aimed at depicting a scenario that reflects reality, whether as it is known at present or as it is known to have existed in the past. An example of *reality-directed imagination* would be the study of Napoleon.

Fantasy-directed imagination attempts to produce a world of make-belief, creating characters and events that have had no concrete existence in reality and are founded on a purely inventive mind. *Reality-directed imagination*, for its part, endeavours to re-create, in the intellectual realm, actions and events that have existed or have taken place, which we may have plenty or partial information about.

Without *Fantasy-directed imagination* our life would be much poorer. Children's literature would not exist; many of the movies we have grown up with would not have been produced; some works of art would never have been created; mythology would be wholly unknown. Without *reality-directed imagination*, on the other hand, the study of history would be well-nigh impossible.

Reality-directed imagination helps us to reconstruct history, to describe it and to understand it.

Reality-directed imagination helps us in the study of history and, in turn, enhances our imaginative abilities. It is both a means to absorb the facts of history and a tool to improve the use of imagination as a reality-directed vehicle.

In the study of history we make use of *reality-directed imagination* as we depict in our minds the characters of individuals or the nature of events. We even try to fill the gaps by resorting to our imagination ever vigilant not to lose sight of reality as it was. In other words, we attempt to imagine the unknown by resorting to the known.

We thus use imagination to recreate what happened and to infer what may have happened. Imagination allows us to link pieces of information into a coherent picture and to understand its significance in a wider context.

By resorting to *reality-directed imagination* we are able intellectually to disconnect ourselves from the present; to visualize, like a landscape gradually making its appearance as we move backwards in time, the setting in which an event occurred or the personal features of an individual we follow. We are able emotionally to connect ourselves to the prevailing conditions or to a person's thoughts. We are able to be there without being there.

Imagination becomes a tool to transport us backwards in time while remaining glued to reality. We let our minds float well above our present, deep into the realm of the past, eschewing, though, the fantastic. *Reality-directed imagination* is thus a means to retain a solid sense of reality rather than to submerge into the everlasting landscape of fantasy. We imagine what was and try to afford it life.

We can transport ourselves to the Escorial and see King Philip II of Spain as he writes a side-note on a state paper; and then take a turn backwards and contemplate how Pope Boniface VIII and King Philip IV of France argue over who should have primary authority over temporal affairs, the Pope or the King; and afterwards turn again forward and follow the Ottoman troops as they advance toward Vienna; and then, in a leisurely manner, accompany Diego Velazquez as he paints the Rendition of Breda.

We can stand next to Viscount Castlereagh as he confers with his European colleagues at the Congress of Vienna in an endeavor to design a new international system; and then set our eyes to the future and watch how Otto von Bismarck smokes a cigar as he contemplates his next diplomatic move aimed at securing the unification of Germany; we can move forward and see Gavrilo Princip as he shoots the Archduke Franz Ferdinand of Austria and his wife Sophie; and then join President Woodrow Wilson at the peace conference in Paris as he exchanges views with Prime Ministers Lloyd George and George Clemenceau in an attempt to set up a new international order; finally, we can sit next to Prime Minister Stanley Baldwin as he meets King Edward VIII to discuss his relationship with Wallis Simpson and the emerging constitutional crisis created as a result.

We can do all that and more, but when we put our thoughts on paper or share them with our students we need to connect the dots, to relate the facts, to explain the background, to describe the circumstances, to understand the motives, to analyze the actions and to assess the repercussions, for which *reality-directed imagination* is vital. Without it, history becomes an incoherent puzzle.

Without imagination as a study-device, the learning of history becomes well-nigh impossible, for the information furnished to us is rendered unintelligible. We are unable to relate to it in any meaningful manner. We assess it in a mechanical way, devoid of image, sound and feel. Our attempt to understand it leads to a dead-end for we cannot leap forward from the stale fact before us and relate it to other facts beyond it. Without imagination we cannot compare, distinguish and separate; we cannot know the difference between the particular and the general. In order to study history we need to avoid the mechanical, on the one hand, and the fantastic, on the other. In other words, we ought to eschew both lack of imagination and *fantasy-directed imagination*; the first does not allow us to proceed forward while the latter leads us to the realm of the unreal.

History is the province both of art and science, of the contemplative and the concrete. To know it, to understand it, to relate to it, we need imagination; an imagination that does not create a new world, but rather re-creates an old one.

Originally published in History News Network, August 7, 2016

Counterfactual History and the Outbreak of World War I

I was an undergraduate student the first time I heard about counterfactual history, and it was in connection with the crisis that led to the outbreak of the Great War, or World War I. I remember a history professor of mine referring with intellectual disdain to the question "What would have happened if Gavrilo Princip had failed to kill the Archduke Franz Ferdinand?" World War I would have erupted in any event, sooner or later, he went on to say. My conclusion, after hearing his comment, was that counterfactual history was intellectually irrelevant if not wholly unacceptable.

Many of my own students today express their dismay when I resort to counterfactual history in my classes. They have been taught that what counts is what actually happened and not what might have happened. They ask, "Isn't the query 'What would have happened if X or Y had not taken place?' beyond the academic domain of the serious historian?"

To be sure, that's exactly what I used to think when I was their age. I no longer do.

In order to argue my case in favor of counterfactual history, I explain to them the difference between science fiction and counterfactual history.

For instance, the question "What would have happened had a meteorite fallen on Gavrilo Princip a few minutes before he managed to kill the Archduke Franz Ferdinand and his wife, Sophie?" is not counterfactual history, but science fiction.

However, the question "What would have happened if Gavrilo Princip had failed in his assassination attempt?" is counterfactual history and not science fiction.

Counterfactual history is not science fiction because it is based on a series of events that *did* happen and asks a question about something that *might have* happened differently. The variables employed are not *fictional*. The assumptions entertained are not *illusory*.

Contrary to what I thought when I was a student, and to what many of my own students believe, counterfactual history is not designed to depict a scenario that *could not* have happened, but rather one that *might have* happened.

The aim is not to change history, as is wrongly assumed. Rather, the objective is to understand it better. In other words, counterfactual history is a device aimed at comprehending better the role of the different actors in the story being studied. Also, it is a means to comprehend the importance of chance or accident in human affairs.

Counterfactual history is anathema to those who believe in historical determinism. After all, if one believes that things are preordained or follow a certain coherent pattern toward a predetermined end, a scenario entailing a different turn of events is unlikely to be entertained lightly. Even if events might be countenanced to have evolved differently than they actually were, their importance in changing historical processes would be discounted.

Counterfactual history is based on the assumption that events are not preordained and that individuals are not actors playing a role without being aware of it. Certainly, circumstances may limit their scope of decision and constrain their freedom of action. However, on the whole, decision makers are thought to be free agents and their decisions the corollary of choice. Counterfactual history would be irrelevant if one were to assume otherwise.

To be sure, the question "What would have happened if X or Y had not occurred?" should not necessarily lead to the depiction of a wholly different scenario from the one that is already known. In other words, one might actually reach the conclusion that the outcome *might have been* similar to the one we know about.

For instance, if we asked what would have happened had Gavrilo Princip failed in his attempt to kill Archduke Franz Ferdinand, and then answered that World War I *might have* erupted anyway, sooner or later, we could still be engaging in counterfactual history.

The "what if" question in this case could lead to an implied conclusion that the role played by Gavrilo Princip in the crisis leading to World War I was not crucial. He was not the *motive* but rather the *instigator* of a process that culminated in the outbreak of World War I. His action was the *trigger* of the crisis that led to war, not its real *cause*. Thus, any other trigger *might have* led to the same outcome, according to this analysis.

Of course, assuming that events *would have* unfolded, in one way or another, in a similar vein could imply a deterministic attitude. Thus, according to this scenario, World War I *would have* erupted with or without the personal intervention of Gavrilo Princip.

In this context, it is important to stress the difference between a *deterministic* and a *probabilistic* analytical perspective. The first negates, whereas the latter allows for contingency. Thus, saying that World War I *would have* occurred anyway denotes a *deterministic* analytical perspective. However, arguing that World War I *might have* occurred reflects a *probabilistic* analytical perspective.

Gavrilo Princip himself is reported to have engaged in counterfactual history. Asked in prison a few years subsequently how he felt about being responsible for the death of so many people, he replied that had he not done what he did Germany would have found another excuse to start the war.

Originally published in Perspectives on History, The Magazine of the American Historical Association, May 1, 2015

There is Counterfactual History as Science and Counterfactual History as Speculation

Is there a way to understand better *what happened* and to narrow down the possibilities of *what might have happened* in history by resorting to counterfactual history?

Could counterfactual history be a means to clarify *what happened* and rule out *what could not have happened* in history?

Can counterfactual history become a solid research device that can help us sharpen our understanding of *what happened* by clarifying the viability of *what might have happened*?

In order to answer these questions, we need to distinguish between two distinct versions of counterfactual history: *Loose Counterfactual History and Tight Counterfactual History.*

A loose counterfactual question allows a change of a variable in the event being studied by introducing an *external* variable, beyond the variables that are an integral part of the story.

For instance, posing a question such as "Would Britain have adopted a different policy towards Nazi Germany had Neville Chamberlain not been appointed as British Prime Minister in 1937?" would constitute a loose counterfactual question.

Why? Because the question entails a change of the story as we know it by assuming a modification of a protagonist in it. Such a modification presupposes that a different person, rather than Neville Chamberlain, could have served as British Prime Minister between 1937 and 1940.

Thus, a variable that is part of the event being studied (in this case, Neville Chamberlain) is altered by introducing an *external* variable that is not part of the event as we know it (a different individual who might have assumed the role of prime minister).

A tight counterfactual question, on the other hand, entails a change in a variable in the event being studied but without introducing an *external* variable that is not an integral part of the same event, and only if such a change is rendered historically coherent and logically plausible by the facts as are known to us.

For instance, posing a question such as "What would have happened had the plot to assassinate Adolf Hitler in July 1944 been successful?" might be an example of a tight counterfactual question.

Why? Because the variable being changed in this question is an *internal* one, which is part of the story as we know it. No *external* variable is introduced in this question. All the facts are true except the outcome presupposed in the question being posed. We know that there was a plot to assassinate Hitler that was actually carried out in July 1944. We know that Hitler was wounded. Thus, the only variable being changed would be the outcome of the plot that was undertaken.

Still, a tight counterfactual question allows for a change of a variable, but only if it fits logically to the event as it actually happened. The change in the variable is *internal*, and must conform to the other variables in the story.

I would argue that a tight counterfactual question represents a more efficient analytical device than a loose counterfactual question both to understand *what happened* and to narrow down the possibilities of *what might have happened*.

In a sense, a tight counterfactual question presupposes posing a question as to whether a counterfactual question can be asked to begin with. One asks a question to know if the question being asked is plausible or not. Only a knowledge of the other pertinent events and decisions and an assessment of their repercussions can allow us to determine whether the counterfactual question being asked is warranted by the other variables in the story or not.

For instance, let us assume that we asked the following question: "Would Britain have lost World War II had the United States not entered the War in December 1941?" What we would need to do is ask whether there was any chance, considering the historical facts that are known to us, that the United States would not have entered the war following

Japan's attack at Pearl Harbor and Germany's declaration of war. In order to answer the question in a historically coherent and logically plausible manner we would need to alter two important variables in the story as it is known to us. First, Japan would have had to refrain from attacking the United States at Pearl Harbor and consequently Germany would have had to refrain from declaring war on the United States. Without changing those two historical facts, the question becomes devoid of historical coherence.

How many variables in the story would we have to change for the question being asked to have had a plausible chance of becoming true?

The moment we are compelled to change more than one variable in the story we cease dealing with *a plausible* alternative scenario.

Even if only one *internal* variable is altered, a tight counterfactual question would be pertinent if the historical facts warrant it.

For instance, if we were to pose the following question, "What would have happened if the United States had decided not to help Israel with the considerable delivery of weapons during the Yom Kippur War in October, 1973?" we would need to ask ourselves whether the historical facts that are known to us render it logically plausible for such a counterfactual scenario to have emerged.

For example, did President Richard Nixon contemplate *not* meeting Israel's urgent requests for

US weapons? Was he in two minds about it? Was there substantial pressure on him within his administration to refuse Israel's request? What had been Nixon's policies toward Israel until then? Was he being asked to agree to something which went considerably against his political instincts or his strategic worldview? These questions would be intended to clarify to us whether the counterfactual question being asked is historically coherent and can thus be advanced.

Tight counterfactual history narrows the plausibility of *what might have been* by asking questions about *what has been.*

A loose counterfactual question endeavors to imagine *the possible.* A tight counterfactual question attempts to enquire the viability of *the probable.*

The difference between a loose counterfactual question and a tight counterfactual question is like the difference between *speculating* what might have happened and *assessing* what might have happened.

By following a methodical and structured form of questioning to assess whether a counterfactual question is plausible and thus acceptable, tight counterfactual history is the closest form of conjecture there is to knowing the truth as it was and as it might have been.

Originally published in History News Network, April 19, 2016

Truth and History: Historical Truth and Historical Narrative

Is there such a thing as objective truth in history? Is history a compilation of narratives advanced by different groups and nations? The influence wielded by historical narratives on international relations is such as to make it imperative to define conceptually the terms concerned and dwell, albeit briefly, on a few cases.

Historical truth is objective by its very nature. It is there, so to speak, to be discovered and unearthed. Certainly, there may be occasions in which the truth cannot be discovered. However, the inability to discover the truth does not negate its objective existence. In this context, a distinction ought to be drawn between Historical truth and interpretation. The first is objective and the latter is subjective. The first refers to a fact, which can be determined as true, at least in principle, by empirical study, whereas the latter entails an explanation of the fact in question. To be sure, the lack of historical truth may lead to an act of inference, accompanied by interpretation, designed to assess what the truth might have been.

Thus, "narratives", a commonly-used catch-phrase, to afford legitimacy to historical interpretations are, at best, an attempt at explaining historical events from a subjective perspective. Their importance resides in the influence they wield in shaping the perception of reality by groups or nations. Narratives may determine historical truth insofar as they describe the perception of groups or nations as they exist objectively, but the historical veracity of the facts which those narratives depict do not derive necessarily from them. They may be objectively true or false.

This is not to belittle the importance of historical narratives. Their emotional impact may determine the manner by which decision-makers interpret the external environment in which they operate, and make decisions affecting the group or nation they represent.

Still, historical narratives are not a synonym for historical truth. However powerful historical narratives may be in shaping the actions of a certain group or nation, they do not, per se, reflect historical truth. A historical narrative may be based on historical truth, but to believe that historical truth may not be objectively determined and thus one is left only with historical narratives is to confuse the objective existence of truth with its subjective interpretation.

The assumption that the subjective interpretation of history is automatically rendered into a historical truth on account of its historical impact is clearly wrong.

We can witness the effects of historical narratives on the nature of contemporary international relations.

Suffice us to glance at the differing narratives by the Turks and the Armenians of the Armenian Genocide and their effects on international relations. Indeed, the term "Armenian Genocide" is part and parcel of the fierce dispute between the two sides about the events surrounding the murder of around one and a half million Armenians by the Ottoman Turks, starting in 1915. While the Armenians contend that the Ottoman Turks perpetrated a well-prepared and thought-out act of genocide, the Turks argue that the Armenians were a hostile element within the Ottoman Empire and that the events concerned reflected a violent conflict between two contending sides, and not an organized effort at genocide. Any attempt by a third party to recognize the Armenian Genocide is immediately followed by strong protests by the Turkish Government. Governments and parliaments assess the pros and cons of recognizing the Armenian Genocide on the basis not only of moral but also of pragmatic considerations as to its effect on bilateral relations with Turkey.

The differing accounts by the Palestinian Arabs and the Israelis about the nature of the Arab-Israeli conflict is a further example of historical narratives that still wield a strong influence on the character of an international conflict. Thus, for instance, the Palestinian Arabs refer to the events surrounding the establishment of the State of Israel as a Nakba, or Catastrophe in Arabic, leading to the displacement of hundreds of thousands of Palestinian Arabs from their homes, whereas the Israelis stress the refusal of the leadership of the Palestinian Arabs to accept the UN Partition Plan of 1947, which could have led to the establishment of a Palestinian Arab state alongside Israel, and their subsequent decision to launch an all-out attack against the Jewish community in Mandatory Palestine, followed by an attack by the Arab countries against the newly-established State of Israel. For the Palestinian Arabs the establishment of Israel led to the Nakba; for the Israelis, the Nakba was the result of the refusal of the Palestinian Arabs to accept a compromise solution and the decision to launch an all-out attack, without which there would have been no war and no refugee problem.

A further example relates to the tensions prevailing between Russia and Poland about the events surrounding the start of the Second World War and the role played by the Soviet Union in it. Russia stresses the role played by the Soviet Union in defeating Nazi Germany and liberating Poland from the yoke of German occupation, while Poland puts as much emphasis on the Ribbentrop-Molotov Pact of August 1939, which stipulated that Poland would be divided between Nazi Germany and the Soviet Union. For Poland, the Soviet Union was as much a liberator as an oppressor.

Historical narratives may reflect historical truth or not. Their aim is not necessarily to ascertain what actually happened in the past, but to justify what happens in the present. Narratives are important to understand the attitudes that form part of the decision-making process of the sides involved in an international dispute. A clear distinction ought to be drawn between historical narratives as a tool to comprehend the mind-setting behind the positions adopted by the sides concerned, and historical truth as such. The historical narrative of one side may reflect historical truth more than the historical narrative of the other. Indeed, in general, one may be subjective and right. Still, conceptually, the two are not necessarily related. Historical truth stands alone, in its own right. Historical narratives may reflect historical truth, but, however influential they may be in historical and contemporary parlance, they occupy a separate place.

Originally published in History News Network, March 6, 2020